Marriage, Divorce, and Children's Adjustment

DEVELOPMENTAL CLINICAL PSYCHOLOGY AND PSYCHIATRY SERIES

Series Editor: **Alan E. Kazdin,** *Western Psychiatric Institute*

In the Series:

Marriage, Divorce, and Children's Adjustment

Robert E. Emery

Volume 14.
Developmental Clinical Psychology and Psychiatry

SAGE PUBLICATIONS
The Publishers of Professional Social Science
Newbury Park   Beverly Hills   London   New Delhi

To Jean and to my parents, Bob and Margaret

For information address:

SAGE Publications, Inc.
2111 West Hillcrest Drive
Newbury Park, California 91320

SAGE Publications Inc.
275 South Beverly Drive
Beverly Hills
California 90212

SAGE Publications Ltd.
28 Banner Street
London EC1Y 8QE
England

SAGE PUBLICATIONS India Pvt. Ltd.
M-32 Market
Greater Kailash I
New Delhi 110 048 India

Printed in the United States of America

Library of Congress Cataloging-in-Publication Data

Main entry under title:

Emery, Robert E.
    Marriage, divorce, and children's adjustment.

    (Developmental clinical psychology and psychiatry;
v. 14)
    Includes bibliographies and index.
    1. Children of divorced parents—Mental health.
2. Adjustment (Psychology) in children.   3. Family—
Psychological aspects.   I. Title.   II. Series.
[DNLM: 1. Adaptation, Psychological—in infancy &
childhood. 2. Divorce. 3. Marriage. 4. Social
Adjustment—in infancy & childhood.   W1 DE997NC
v. 14/
WS 105.5.A8 E53m]
RJ507.D59E44   1987   155.4   87–26502
ISBN 0–8039–2780–0
ISBN 0–8039–2781–9 (pbk.)

CONTENTS

SERIES EDITOR'S INTRODUCTION

Interest in child development and adjustment is by no means new. Yet, only recently has the study of children benefited from advances in both clinical and scientific research. Advances in the social and biological sciences, the emergence of disciplines and subdisciplines that focus exclusively on childhood and adolescence, and greater appreciation of the impact of such influences as the family, peers, and school have helped accelerate research on developmental psychopathology. Apart from interest in the study of child development and adjustment for its own sake, the need to address clinical problems of adulthood naturally draws one to investigate precursors in childhood and adolescence.

Within a relatively brief period, the study of psychopathology among children and adolescents has proliferated. Several different professional journals, annual book series, and handbooks devoted entirely to the study of children and adolescents and their adjustment, document the proliferation of work in the field. Nevertheless, there is a paucity of resource material that presents information in an authoritative, systematic, and disseminable manner. There is a need within the field to convey the latest developments and to present the various disciplines, approaches, and conceptual views pertaining to childhood and adolescent adjustment and maladjustment.

The Sage Series *Developmental Clinical Psychology and Psychiatry* is uniquely designed to serve several needs of the field. The Series encompasses individual monographs prepared by experts in the fields of clinical child psychology, child psychiatry, child development, and related disciplines. The primary focus is on developmental psychopathology, which refers broadly here to the diagnosis, assessment, treatment, and prevention of problems arising in the period from infancy through adolescence. A working assumption of the Series is that understanding, identifying, and treating problems of youth must draw on multiple disciplines and diverse views within a given discipline.

The task for individual contributors is to present the latest theory and research on various topics, including specific types of dysfunction, diagnostic and treatment approaches, and special problem areas that affect adjustment. Core topics within clinical work are addressed by the Series. Authors are asked to bridge potential theory, research, and clinical practice, and to outline the current status and future directions of their speciality. The goals of the Series and the tasks presented to individual contributors are demanding. We have been extremely fortunate in recruiting leaders in the fields who have been able to translate their recognized scholarship and expertise into highly readable works on contemporary topics.

The present book, prepared by Dr. Robert Emery, focuses on *Marriage, Divorce, and Children's Adjustment*. The topic is one of obvious significance because of the social significance of marriage and divorce and the pivotal role of the family in the development and adjustment of children. In the present monograph Dr. Emery provides a concise, albeit extremely comprehensive, treatment of the topic. He integrates and evaluates research on separation, divorce, custody relations, divorce settlement, and remarriage, and the impact of these on children and parents. Alternative interventions for children, parents, and families are also discussed. The perspective is broad and draws upon historical, cross-cultural, interpersonal, psychological, legal, and economic facets of marital dissolution. Sufficient work has been completed to provide statistics on divorce and the impact of marital conflict on children and their families. The unique features of this book are its comprehensive treatment of the topic and an unusually clear and incisive evaluation of current findings.

—*Alan E. Kazdin, Ph.D.*
Series Editor

PREFACE

Some bemoan the disappearance of the "traditional" family while others simultaneously cheer the new diversity in acceptable family forms. Children of divorced parents are portrayed as either fragile or magnificently resilient. In the din over which extreme view is right, much useful, reasonably adequate empirical evidence is often overlooked. Unfortunately, so are many individual children and families. We must not be insensitive to the difficult transitions that divorce entails for most families, at least in the short-term. Neither should we unjustly assume that the long-term outcome of divorce is inevitably pathological.

In this book, I attempt to avoid the polemics of either extreme while setting forth both the normative evidence and depicting the individual child or family. I have conducted sufficient research on marital conflict and divorce to know that empirical information is limited, and have confronted these limits more directly in innumerable therapy and mediation sessions. Still, we are not operating in a vacuum. A lot of work has been done, and much of it is relevant to intervention in divorce, whether at the clinical or the policy level.

Evidence from both the research and the clinical domain is integrated here, although the emphasis is clearly on the former. I consider such attempts at integration as one of the tasks of the scientist-practitioner. Clinical experience is invaluable for generating ideas for research, empirical information is necessary to inform clinical practice, and success in both the clinical and the research enterprise requires objective observers who can develop clear hypotheses and test them systematically.

The clinician-researcher interface also demands more academic activities related to the evaluation and integration of evidence from both inside and outside psychology. In writing this book, one of the most exciting intellectual tasks has been the exposure not only to the research and practice of psychology, but also of such diverse fields as history, sociology, economics, and law. Hopefully, these varied perspectives will also engage and challenge the reader. I suspect that in the future there will be fewer disciplinary approaches to studying human behavior and greater integration of life and social sciences within particular substantive areas.

I wish to thank a number of people for their assistance in helping me write this book. Elizabeth Scott, Frank Furstenberg, and the Series editor, Alan Kazdin, each provided valuable feedback on drafts of the manuscript. My colleague Mavis Hetherington has been a resource, advocate, and tough critic. My colleagues at the University of Virginia with interests in psychology and law have expanded my horizons immensely. These include Elizabeth Scott, Walter Wadlington, Dick Reppucci, and John Monahan. I would also like to thank those people who have helped me learn about legal realities, as well as legal theory. These include members of the "mediation team" at the Charlottesville Juvenile and Domestic Relations Court, Joanne Jackson, Judge Ralph Zehler, Jr., "Cookie" Scott, and many hard-working graduate students, too numerous to name. Financial support has been provided by the William T. Grant Foundation, the Harry Frank Guggenheim Foundation, and the Center for Advanced Studies at the University of Virginia. Finally, I would like to thank my wife, Jean, and my daughter, Maggie, for their patience and support when I was working early in the morning or late at night.

—*Robert E. Emery*
Charlottesville, Virginia

1

INTRODUCTION

If there is one thing that can be said to characterize all divorces, it is change. Some changes begin well before the physical separation, others continue long after the legal divorce. Changes in the family can result in an improved or a worsened environment, but they do require that children adapt to them. Thus, the psychological impact of divorce on children must be considered on at least two levels. The first is the process of adaptation to change that every child must go through. Apparently, the fewer disruptions a divorce entails and the more quickly a new stability is achieved, the less stressful this process of adaptation will be.

The second level of psychological impact divorce has on children concerns their long-term adjustment. The stability reached in the postdivorce family environment may be better, worse, or merely different from that which existed before the divorce. Particular patterns of family interaction, as well as various characteristics of the children, seem to be associated with more positive or more negative long-term outcomes.

In considering how children cope with divorce, the difficulties that are typically involved in the process of adaptation should not be minimized, while the frequency with which the family transition leads to abnormal outcomes must not be overstated. Divorce has become a very common event in the United States. To suggest that its impact on children is inevitably pathological is an injustice to a great number of families. To suggest that divorce is an insignificant transition reveals insensitivity. Perhaps what is most insensitive and unjust, is to arrive at conclusions about divorce and its effects on children without carefully considering what we know, not just what we believe.

GAINING PERSPECTIVE ON CHILDREN AND DIVORCE

It is difficult to gain perspective on assumptions about a subject that is such a prominent social concern, and for many, a very personal one. Our views about children and divorce force all of us to examine our beliefs about the family and child-rearing. Indeed, a discussion of the consequences of divorce is senseless without a consideration of views about "normal" families and "healthy" child-rearing.

It is not just individuals who find it difficult to gain perspective on divorce. Due to certain assumptions made in a particular field of study, entire professional disciplines may develop a restricted view of divorce. Mental health professionals have traditionally focused on the individual as the unit of analysis. This directs the search for the causes and consequences of divorce "within the skin" of the individual. Because of this conceptual approach, external events are often reduced in significance largely to their psychological meaning.

The individual perspective can be of considerable value, but its value is enhanced if children and divorce are viewed from other perspectives as well. Psychologists, legal professionals, economists, sociologists, anthropologists, and historians all have different perspectives on divorce, which reflect professional assumptions about the appropriate level of analysis. No one view is "right." Rather, each level of conceptualization is nested within increasingly broader levels of abstraction. For example, a psychologist may view noncompliance with child-support awards as stemming from a former husband's unresolved marital hostility. A lawyer may see the same problem as the fault of a judge, who should enforce support awards more stringently. An economist might cite the need to connect child-support payments with visitation rights. A sociologist might note the continuing economic inequities for women in American society. An anthropologist may suggest that child-rearing is supported in different cultures in different ways. Finally, an historian might view the problem as a part of the incomplete evolution of familial and social support structures.

It is possible that each view may be correct—or incorrect. Like the telescope, compared to the microscope, these diverse disciplines offer different lenses through which children and divorce can be viewed. Examining the subject from different levels of analysis is likely to result in a more thorough understanding of marriage, divorce, and children.

SOME FAMILY TRANSITIONS IN DIVORCE

Until recent years, much psychological literature was devoted to discussions of subtle aspects of children's conceptions of and reactions to divorce. Ironically, part of the reason for the focus on psychological complexity was that divorce was viewed simplistically. Many authors conceptualized divorce as a uniform psychological event rather than a process that may or may not entail various social, psychological, and economic changes.

Contemporary researchers are much more concerned with the process of divorce and the changes it entails. Children are often exposed to parental conflict before the divorce, in the courtroom itself, and in postdivorce family life. Because children are a tie between divorced partners, unresolved anger over the marriage can be channeled into disputes about child-rearing. Most children also feel the pressures created by torn loyalties even when parents cooperate relatively well.

Divorce likewise causes children to lose contact with one parent, typically their father. The resulting separation distress may be prolonged for unpredictable periods of time as the possibility of a marital reconciliation is kept alive and trial separations are attempted. What is predictable is that the amount of contact between the children and one parent will be greatly diminished.

The need for a new job and a new social life may also result in residential parents being physically less available to their children. The burden of becoming a single parent may lead to their being psychologically less available as well. Out of necessity, some parents adopt higher expectations for their children following divorce. Role strain or preoccupation with their own emotional state may cause others to be less nurturant and harsher disciplinarians. The opposite behavior may result from guilt, self-doubt, or limited contact with the children.

Financial trouble is a change that is hardly subtle to members of divorced families. Children may be forced to move from the family home and to change schools or child-care placements due to a decline in their standard of living. Divorced mothers often must re-evaluate and redefine the roles they assumed in marriage, as they seek employment for the first time, try to find better paying jobs, or apply for public assistance. While their financial circumstances are better on the average, fathers may feel that the divorce has reduced their paternal role to one that is measured solely in terms of dollars.

Finally, children are likely to face a new challenge at some time after the divorce: the remarriage of one or of both their parents. A remarriage may rekindle parental anger, further reduce contact with the nonresidential parent, or introduce a stepparent and perhaps stepsiblings into the household. A stepparent may become a new source of support for the children, or he or she may be viewed as an intruder and rival.

These are some of the significant events that seem to demand at least as much attention as psychological subtleties. Indeed, the fact that most children successfully cope with the myriad changes that divorce entails is a measure of their resilience.

AN OVERVIEW OF THIS BOOK

While the primary focus of this book is psychological research, for the reasons outlined above, evidence and perspectives from other social sciences are also offered. These perspectives sometimes challenge psychological assumptions about child development and child psychopathology. In turn, the perspective offered by another discipline may be incomplete or lack focus, and the psychological research is illuminating.

In focusing on psychological research, no single theoretical perspective has been adopted. Neither is this review atheoretical. Divorce is a multifactorial process, and no one theory of development can adequately account for its multiple potential influences. There are areas where competing theoretical views can be contrasted, however. In such circumstances, alternative predictions are examined and critically evaluated.

Although most of the research discussed here emphasizes the psychological aspects of family relationships, an attempt is made to consider some of the additional functions that families fulfill. American couples may marry for love, but their union serves many other purposes. In addition to nurturing and socializing children, families provide for their members' economic support and help to educate children and define their roles in the larger community. Like more direct child-care responsibilities, these family functions are often disrupted by divorce. Such changes can impact on children's psychological development directly, or indirectly by affecting family relationships.

In reviewing current evidence on children and divorce, this book begins with broader perspectives, moves toward increasingly individualized discussion, and returns again to a broad overview. In Chapter 2, some cross-cultural and historical differences in the definition of families are noted, a brief history of children and divorce is sketched, and a rather detailed demographic portrait of contemporary divorce is outlined. In Chapter 3, some conceptual and methodological problems which characterize research on children and divorce are discussed. Chapter 4 is an overview of normative evidence on the effects of divorce based on studies comparing the average adjustment of children from married and divorced families. Chapter 5 is more concerned with individual differences, presenting evidence on the processes that predict various outcomes of divorce for children. Some idiographic, clinical perspectives on the psychological adjustment and treatment of members of divorcing and divorced families are considered in Chapter 6. Finally, in Chapter 7, legal interventions in divorce are reviewed in the light of existing research findings, which help to define the goals of social policy.

2

SOME CULTURAL, HISTORICAL, AND DEMOGRAPHIC PERSPECTIVES

Some views on families and divorce are examined here from the broad perspectives of anthropology, history, and sociology. This brief review serves several purposes in setting the stage for a discussion of more focused psychological research in later chapters. Historical and sociological research helps to define a context in which current social, legal, and psychological assumptions about the family can be appreciated. In addition, the demographic literature confronts us with realities about the prevalence of divorce in the United States today, and the influence of factors such as age, race, income, and children themselves.

Perhaps most importantly, a consideration of families across cultures and time indicates that it is a mistake to think about the family as a single, fixed entity. Rather, both anthropologists and historians have pointed out that family forms and functions adapt according to the requirements of the larger society. Since the definition of family depends upon broader social supports and demands, so does the meaning of divorce. Divorce can be expected to have quite different consequences for children depending upon the "family" functions fulfilled by other social structures.

The impact of divorce on children, therefore, depends partially on the child-rearing supports offered outside the family. For this reason, the possibility of offering assistance to children of divorce is not unfounded. This conclusion raises an important question for both historians and current social policy makers. When state and other extrafamilial agencies offer increased child-rearing support, is this a cause or a consequence of changes in the family? If increased support from governmental or other social agencies causes the family to change, an argument for minimal intervention could be made, since such support could be construed as undermining the family. In contrast, if increased state support is an attempt to fill important gaps created by family forms that are changing for other reasons, then intervention from the larger community would seem to be in order. In this case, outside agencies may be seen as attempting to supplement rather than to supplant traditional child-rearing functions, perhaps as part of a further historical redefinition of "family."

THE CHANGING FAMILY

Contrary to the view that the two-parent nuclear family is "normal" and "healthy," some political advocates have suggested that the definition of "family" is not necessarily two parents with a son and a daughter. Rather, it is argued that family is defined by a pattern of relationships. This view is consistent with the findings of anthropologists, who have noted the variety of family forms found in various cultures. It is also supported by those historians who have suggested that the Western family is a continually evolving system, one that responds to changing social and economic demands.

Divorce in Two Tribal Societies

In the early 1950s, divorce rates among the Hadza, a hunter-gatherer society in eastern Africa, were five times greater than in the United States. After divorce, a father typically moved to reside with a different band of Hadza, while the children remained with their mother. Like children who had a biological father in residence, Hadza children of divorce were cared for emotionally and economically by all members of their small band, a population which continually changed and intermingled with other bands (Bilge & Kaufman, 1983).

Among the Hopi Indians of the American Southwest, in the early part of the twentieth century, 66% of all first marriages were estimated to end in divorce. In this matriarchal society, women and their male and female relatives were charged with the primary responsibility for child-care irrespective of whether the marriage was intact or not. Following divorce, children therefore remained in the care of their mothers. Divorced fathers returned to reside with their own mothers but could freely visit their biological children (Bilge & Kaufman, 1983).

In the Hadza and Hopi cultures, separation and divorce were not considered detrimental to children. In fact, divorce did not greatly change the life experiences of children. No stigma was associated with it, and social structures were such that marital dissolution minimally disrupted the family's material resources and social support (Bilge & Kaufman, 1983).

This consideration of divorce in cultures so radically different from American society may seem irrelevant. This, in fact, is the point. It is obvious that the consequences of divorce differ in very different societies; it is equally obvious that we are not discussing universal laws here, when we consider the effects of divorce per se. Much of the research about the consequences of divorce for American children must be bound by culture and time. At another point in history or in another culture, divorce might lead to quite different life events and, therefore, to different psychological outcomes. For similar reasons, divorce can be expected to have different consequences for children living within various subcultures in contemporary American society.

A consideration of divorce in diverse cultures also indicates that the consequences of divorce for children cannot be fully understood by focusing solely on the event of divorce. While the fact that their parents have divorced is a point of similarity across cultures, the wide range of social consequences makes the children of divorce at least as different as they are alike. Marital dissolution does not result in the same life changes for children in different cultures, nor does it result in the same life changes for different children within the same culture. When the emphasis is shifted from the event of divorce per se to the changes in family life that it may entail, not only is cultural diversity apparent, but individual differences are also highlighted.

While diversity is important to recognize, so is similarity. As discussed in Chapters 4 and 5, despite considerable variations, there are enough consequences of divorce common to American children to allow some generalizations to be made. Unlike the Hadza and Hopi cultures, divorce in the United States typically leads to considerable temporary disruption in children's intra- and extrafamilial support systems. Lasting disruptions are found among a smaller proportion of divorced families. Simply put, unlike what is found in some other cultures, divorce is not an innocuous event for most children living in the United States today.

Changing Structure of the Western Family

Interest in the history of childhood and family has increased in recent years as social scientists have attempted to gain a better perspective on contemporary family forms. A brief examination of this history would be useful since many ideas about what is wrong with divorce stem from notions about what is right with the two-parent family. But from the historical perspective, one must either conclude that child-rearing throughout important periods in Western history was pathogenic, or that assumptions about what constitutes a healthy family are questionable (Kagan, 1985). In general, historical transformations reinforce the view that there is not just one acceptable family form, but several.

The structure of the Western family has undergone continual change, albeit a very gradual one, as family size has decreased from bands and tribes to extended families to nuclear families (Aries, 1962). Historians speculate that the extended, patriarchal family developed from tribal organization as a result of changing economic conditions. This new family form served as a means of preserving the property and social status that accompanied the development of agriculture, the domestication of animals, and the breeding of herds (Engels, 1942, 1970). While the emergence of the nuclear family may predate the Industrial Revolution (Harever, 1986), industrialization and urbanization seem to have facilitated the further reduction in size of the Western family. Labor demands were fulfilled more effectively by the smaller nuclear family with its more specialized roles (Goode, 1968).

The steadily increasing divorce rate over the past hundred years and the rise in out-of-wedlock births (see below) would seem to constitute a continuation of this historical shrinkage of the family. Because of evolving economic conditions and child-rearing supports, the specialized roles of breadwinner and caretaker that characterize the "traditional" nuclear family may be less of a financial necessity than they once were. The individual worker, or more likely, the dual earner household, may become a unit that rivals the nuclear family in meeting economic demands. As male and female family roles become more supplementary than complementary, and as further child-rearing supports are developed to aid workers, divorce becomes a greater possibility, albeit one that contains incentives for eventual remarriage. In general, the workplace increasingly seems to be the unit around which relationships are organized. In this regard, legal scholar Mary Ann Glendon (1980) has made an intriguing observation. She has noted that while laws regulating the ties between husband and wife have become less restrictive, laws tying the company to the worker have become more restrictive.

Predicting the future of the family is highly speculative, but it is evident that Western family forms have not remained constant. Family structures have changed according to broader social demands. From this perspective it would seem that, in the absolute sense, the nuclear family is more idealized than ideal. Nevertheless, the notion that family structure is an adaptive response to the demands of the larger society also means that, in the relative sense, the nuclear family is suited to meet the demands of contemporary society. As implied by the work of anthropologists and historians and documented by research on the consequences of divorce, the two-parent nuclear family effectively fulfills a number of functions. As suggested above, other family forms may gradually come to be equally or more adaptive.

Family Functions

As the structure of the Western family has changed, so have its functions. Prior to the Industrial Revolution, the family was expected to fulfill most, if not all, of its members' needs. Family functions included protecting its members and providing them with economic support; offering educational and religious training; providing affection and recreation for its members; and serving to define a role in the larger community (Ogburn, 1953; Parsons, 1968). As society became increasingly centralized, state agencies such as factories, schools, churches, and police assumed increasing responsibility for many of these functions. Offering affection to its members and socializing children remained, perhaps, the most autonomous family responsibilities.

Since the late nineteenth century, the state has been given an increasingly important role in supplementing or replacing even these last two functions. The legal concept of *parens patriae*, the state as parent, brought about radical changes in the juvenile justice system, with the concept of rehabilitation replacing punishment. Houses of Refuge, reformatories, and child-guidance clinics were created in an attempt to save children from deprived homes and inadequate parenting (Empey, 1976). While the telescopic view of history becomes less focused with a foreshortening of time, it would seem that efforts in the twentieth century to provide more state-supported care, education, and economic support for children are consistent with this historical trend. State agencies have increasingly assumed functions that were once exclusively the domain of the family in its various forms.

State Assumption of Family Functions: Impetus for, or Response to, Family Change?

While the historical trends seem clear, they should not be over-stated. Family size has decreased and social agencies have assumed a greater voice in family functions, but the state is hardly an adequate substitute parent. The truth of this statement becomes apparent when marriages are dissolved. The fact that economic support, educational opportunities, the definition of social roles, affectional relationships, and the socialization of children can all suffer as a result of divorce, indicates that the nuclear family independently fulfills a number of functions.

Whether the state *should* be available to serve as a family surrogate is debatable. Controversy centers on how many "family" functions the state can and should provide. Empirically, this debate often takes the form of differences of opinion about the consequences of making state support available. Some argue that state support serves as a disincentive for families to fulfill their traditional child-rearing functions. From this perspective, increased support for divorced families has the unwanted side effect of serving as a disincentive to marriage. Others counter that the disincentive to marriage incurred by state support for divorced and single-parent families is insignificant. Rather, state programs are thought to fill the gap left when children's needs are unmet for other reasons.

Whether state policies are a cause of changes in family structure or a response to the needs of new family forms is therefore not only debated by academics but hotly contested by social policy makers. For example, questions have been raised about what impact state-guaranteed financial support for dependent children has on marital dissolution.

In fact, contemporary experimental and correlational data are available on precisely this issue. Evidence from the Denver and Seattle income-maintenance experiments indicates that state financial support may have a dramatic effect on separation/divorce rates. Increases of 50% or greater in the rate of separation/divorce were noted among families assigned at random to receive temporarily guaranteed incomes above what was available through the usual Aid to Families with Dependent Children (AFDC) payments and food stamp supplements (Groeneveld, Hannan, & Tuma, 1983; Hannan, Tuma, & Groeneveld, 1977).

While the experimental manipulation used in the income-maintenance studies clearly demonstrated the causal impact of increased AFDC awards on marital dissolution rates, estimates of the extent of the effect may have been distorted. The time-limited nature of the experiments may have produced an exaggerated short-time increase in the rates, as unhappily married couples were encouraged to separate quickly while the increased income was still available. Moreover, the experimental subjects in these studies received support payments above what was normally provided. Marital disruption rates may have been exaggerated by unrealistically high payments. In support of both these possibilities, a correlation between higher AFDC payments and higher separation/divorce rates was found in a recent study comparing states that offer various payment levels, but estimates of the magnitude of the effect were much more modest (Elwood & Bane, 1985). State financial support encourages (or allows for) increased rates of separation/divorce, but the effects may be much smaller than some have assumed.

The income-maintenance experiments are unusual in that they are direct, experimental studies of a social policy. All too often the evidence that researchers provide policy makers is indirect and correlational. Even when experimental designs are employed to address social policy debates, the estimated magnitude of the effect may be open to question, as illustrated above. While there may be no simple answers to the questions posed, such investigations are nonetheless vital for providing information that will help direct social policy. Divorce, children, and social policy are considered in greater detail in Chapter 7.

A BRIEF HISTORY OF MARITAL DISSOLUTION IN THE UNITED STATES

Legal History

Like the AFDC controversy, whether laws governing divorce are a reaction to, or a cause of, changes in the family is a debatable point.

While there is no doubt that legal constraints served as a disincentive to divorce at earlier points in history, many changes in divorce law, particularly in this century, seem to have followed rather than preceded changes in the family.

Until the sixteenth century, divorce in Europe was a religious matter that could be granted on only three grounds: adultery, cruelty, or heresy (Scanzoni, 1979). Following the Reformation, marriage and divorce gradually came under civil control. In the American colonies, marriage and divorce were controlled by the government in the Puritan settlements of the North from the time they were established, whereas religious control was the rule, albeit temporarily, in the South (Halem, 1981).

If divorce was virtually nonexistent when marriage was under the control of the church, available data suggest that it remained exceedingly rare as the state assumed authority. For example, from 1692 till 1786 a total of only 229 divorce petitions were filed in the colony of Massachusetts (Scanzoni, 1979). While the permissible grounds for obtaining a divorce were broadened somewhat, the state was far from encouraging couples to freely enter into and dissolve marriages. Laws governing divorce were strict and designed to discourage divorce by making the "exit costs" high (Halem, 1981; Mnookin, 1975; Weitzman, 1981). One party had to be proven to be at fault in order for a divorce to be granted, and evidence supporting the grounds for finding fault had to be presented to the court. Throughout the nineteenth century it was more difficult for a husband than a wife to be found at fault (Halem, 1981).

As the twentieth century progressed, the judiciary began to interpret narrowly defined legal statutes more broadly in order to accommodate the increasing numbers of people filing for divorce. This is evident in the changing grounds listed in divorce decrees, as the proportion of divorces granted on specific grounds declined. According to the best available national data, between the two periods of 1867–86 and 1965, the following changes occurred: Adultery declined as grounds for 24.6% of all divorces granted in 1867–86 to only 1.4% of all divorces granted in 1965; desertion declined as grounds for divorce from 44.1% to 13.8%; and drunkenness decreased from 7.8% to 0.3%. Concomitantly, the percentage of divorces granted on the vaguer grounds of cruelty increased from 16.3% to 41.7% (Plateris, 1974).

While judicial practice became less restrictive during the twentieth century, no truly dramatic changes in legislative policy occurred until the state of California adopted the first "no fault" divorce law in 1970. Under this new law, one spouse could dissolve the marriage without proving grounds for divorce and even without obtaining the partner's consent. No-fault divorce laws have since been enacted by all 50 states, although some states require both partners to agree, and others have retained fault divorce as an option (Freed & Walker, 1986).

Although it represents a dramatic change in family law, the passage of no-fault laws has not been found to be strongly associated with subsequent increases in the rate of marital dissolution. No dramatic changes in divorce rates followed the passage of no-fault laws on a state-by-state basis in the 1970s (Wright & Stetson, 1978). Thus, there appears to have been a change in family law away from the more activist approach of trying to prevent divorce through strict regulation, to a more passive approach of changing laws in response to altered social circumstances. Contemporary changes in divorce law appear to be an effect, not a cause, of changes in divorce rates.

Demographic History

Consistent with this conclusion, demographics suggest that the increasing incidence of divorce in the United States in the 1960s and 1970s, which has been the focus of so much attention, may reflect a broad historical trend over the last 100 years rather than a recent development (Cherlin, 1981). In 1867, the first year for which national divorce data were available, the annual divorce rate was 0.3 divorces per 1,000 population; at its contemporary peak in 1979 and 1981, the rate was more than 17 times higher or 5.3 per 1,000 population (Glick & Lin, 1986). As shown in Figure 2.1, the frequency of divorce has, by and large, steadily increased from 1867 to 1985.

There are notable exceptions to this trend. For example, the dramatic but transient surge in divorce that followed World War II was not topped until the 1970s. There have also been periods during which the rate declined. Divorce rates dropped during the Depression years, another indication of the economic incentive to remain married. The stabilization or slight decline in divorce rates in the early 1980s may be a similar response to the severe recession of this period. A final trend worth noting is the decline in divorce that occurred during the 1950s. Cherlin (1981) has suggested that this was an *atypical* time in American family history, during which the two-

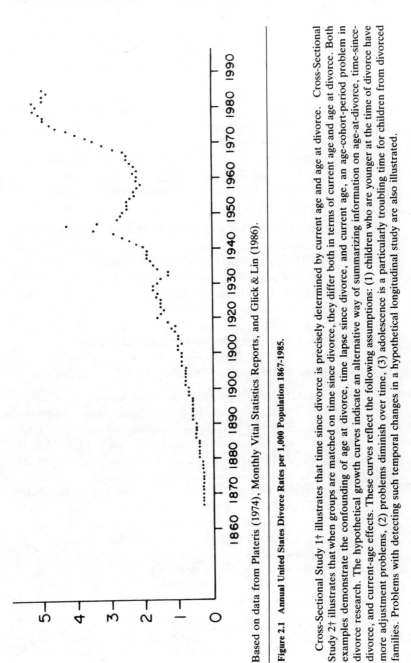

Based on data from Plateris (1974), Monthly Vital Statistics Reports, and Glick & Lin (1986).

Figure 2.1   Annual United States Divorce Rates per 1,000 Population 1867-1985.

Cross-Sectional Study 1† illustrates that time since divorce is precisely determined by current age and age at divorce.   Cross-Sectional Study 2† illustrates that when groups are matched on time since divorce, they differ both in terms of current age and age at divorce. Both examples demonstrate the confounding of age at divorce, time lapse since divorce, and current age, an age-cohort-period problem in divorce research. The hypothetical growth curves indicate an alternative way of summarizing information on age-at-divorce, time-since-divorce, and current-age effects. These curves reflect the following assumptions: (1) children who are younger at the time of divorce have more adjustment problems, (2) problems diminish over time, (3) adolescence is a particularly troubling time for children from divorced families. Problems with detecting such temporal changes in a hypothetical longitudinal study are also illustrated.

parent nuclear family was idealized. He argues that the divorce rates of the 1960s and 1970s were not abnormally high given historical trends; rather, he suggests that the divorce rate of the 1950s was unusually low.

Overall, it is difficult to attribute this long-term rise in the rate of marital dissolution to no-fault divorce, the turbulent sixties, or the "me generation." While there is no doubt that current divorce rates are very high, they must have been influenced by evolving cultural and economic conditions, in addition to contemporary events. Like the evidence for historical changes in the family, this underscores the importance of considering divorce in a broader cultural context.

DEMOGRAPHICS OF DIVORCE IN THE UNITED STATES TODAY

Turning from the past to the future, the question arises as to what percentage of today's couples will eventually divorce. Glick (1984) has projected that fully 49% of those people aged 25 to 34 in 1980 will have their first marriage end in divorce. But divorce rates for the entire population of the United States can obscure important differences between various subgroups of the population.

Some Influences on Divorce Rates

Divorce rates differ dramatically according to race, age, and socioeconomic status. Blacks are more likely to divorce than whites, but blacks are particularly more likely to separate and live apart from their spouse without a legal divorce (Norton & Glick, 1979). Age at first marriage, education, and income are all inversely related to the likelihood of divorce. Age is particularly salient, as divorce rates are twice as high for men who marry before age 20 and for women who marry before age 18 (Norton & Glick, 1979). An interesting observation about education and divorce is that the relation is not a simple linear one. Graduation from high school or college is linked with lower divorce rates than is partial completion of either educational experience, perhaps suggesting a personality characteristic linked both with completing school and remaining married (Glick, 1984).

Divorce is likely to be followed by remarriage. Statistics indicate that five out of six divorced men and three out of four divorced women remarry (Cherlin, 1981). These figures are based on the remarriage rates of earlier generations (older cohorts), however, and at least one demographer has predicted that remarriage rates will be 5.0 to 10.0% lower for the current divorced population (Glick, 1984). Sex differences in the rate of remarriage are attributable to the fact that men are more likely than women to have a younger and never-married second spouse. It is also important to note that remarriage rates among whites are considerably higher than they are among blacks, although exact census data are unavailable (Norton & Glick, 1979).

Children's influence on divorce rates. An important influence on the likelihood of divorce is the presence of children. Today's couples are not as likely to remain married "for the children's sake." Between 1950 and 1965 the proportion of divorces involving children rose from 44% to 60%, and approximately 60% of all divorces continue to involve children (Bane, 1979; Bumpass & Rindfuss, 1979). Evidence does indicate that couples with children are somewhat less likely to divorce than are childless couples (Waite, Haggstrom, & Kanouse, 1985), but the presence of children is not a deterrent in all situations.

Children's age is one important qualifying consideration, as divorce rates for families in which there is a preschool child are about half of what they are for childless families (Waite et al., 1985). For families with children of school age, however, divorce rates are about equal to the rates for childless couples (Cherlin, 1977). The number of children in the family also is related to the likelihood of divorce. Divorce rates are considerably lower for families in which there are one or two children, but families with three or more children have divorce rates which approach those of childless couples (Thornton, 1977). Finally, there are instances in which the presence of children is related to an *increased* likelihood of divorce. Divorce rates are higher when a marriage is preceded by a premarital pregnancy or out-of-wedlock birth (O'Connell & Rogers, 1984), and when step-children are part of a remarriage (White & Booth, 1985).

While children serve as a deterrent under some circumstances, nevertheless a great number of children of the present generation will experience a divorce. They are more or less likely to do so depending on their race and age, and perhaps on their sex.

Family Living Circumstances of Children in the United States Today

The 1982 family living circumstances of American children under age 18 are summarized in Table 2.1. Prepared for the United States

TABLE 2.1

Family Status of Children Under Age 18 Living in the United States in 1982

	All Races	White	Black
Percent living with			
Two parents	75.0%	80.8%	42.4%
Biological parents	63.0%	—	—
One biological and one stepparent	10.0%	—	—
Adoptive parents	2.0%	—	—
Mother only	20.0%	15.3%	47.2%
Divorced	8.2%	8.0%	9.6%
Separated	5.6%	4.3%	13.6%
Never married	4.4%	1.6%	20.8%
Widowed	1.8%	1.5%	3.3%
Father only	1.9%	1.9%	2.0%
Neither parent	3.1%	2.0%	8.4%

Children living with neither parent include those living with other relatives, with nonrelatives, and in institutions.

Based on data from Select Committee on Children, Youth, and Families. *U.S. children and their families: Current conditions and recent trends.* U.S. Government Printing Office. Washington: 1983.

House of Representatives Select Committee on Children, Youth, and Families (SCCYF, 1983), these data indicate that in 1982, 63% of all children in the United States were living with their two biological parents, 10% lived with a biological parent and a stepparent, 20% resided with their mother only, 1.9% lived with their father only, 2.0% lived with two adoptive parents, and 3.1% lived in other family circumstances. The dramatic differences in the family living situations of black and white children are readily evident in this table. While over 80% of all white children were living in a two-parent family, only about half as many black children were. The most dramatic difference in the single-parent living arrangements of black and white children is the percentage living with a never-married mother (20.8%

of black children compared to 1.6% of white children). Even though they were less likely to be born to married parents, about twice as many black as white children also lived with a mother who had been divorced or separated (23.2% vs. 12.3%).

Important aspects concerning children's experience of marital disruption cannot be extracted from census data because they are not sufficiently detailed. Three thorough demographic studies allow for closer inspection of the topic, however. The first is an analysis by Bumpass and Rindfuss (1979) of data from the 1973 Family Growth Survey (FGS), a national probability sample of 9,797 women under the age of 45 who had ever married or were unmarried mothers. The second is the National Survey of Children (NSC) by Zill, Furstenberg and colleagues, a national probability sample of 2,279 children aged seven to eleven living in the 48 contiguous states (Furstenberg et al., 1983). The third study is a replication by Bumpass (1984a) of his earlier work. Based on the June 1980 Current Population Survey, this study is considered in less detail than the other two, except in cases of notable discrepancies.

Summaries from the FGS and NSC on the likelihood of children of different ages and races experiencing a divorce are presented in Table 2.2. The data are divided into two different birth cohorts in order to capture the influence of rising divorce rates during the 1960s. A number of trends discussed above are also evident in these data. A large percentage of American children have experienced a parental divorce, and this percentage has increased among those born in more recent years. According to the NSC, one-quarter of all children born in 1965–67 experienced a parental divorce by the age of 12; in the 1968–69 cohort, the percentage rose dramatically to one-third. Since the annual rate of divorce continued to rise in the years following the birth of the children in these samples, an even greater proportion of children born in the 1970s and 1980s can be expected to experience a divorce. As Furstenberg et al. (1983) have noted, the NSC data suggest that the projection made by Glick (1979) that one-third of all children born in the 1970s will experience a parental divorce by the age of 18 may well be an *under*estimate. Indeed, based on the replication study with a later-born cohort, Bumpass (1984a) suggested that 38% of all white and 75% of all black children born to married parents will experience a divorce before the age of 16.

At least one more observation, one all too often passed over by both demographers and psychologists, should be noted about the

TABLE 2.2

Cumulative Proportion[1] of Children Experiencing Marital Disruption

	Child's Age at Time of Disruption															
	1	2	3	4	5	6	7	8	9	10	11	12	13	14	15	16
Cohort																
All Children																
FGS: 1965–67	5	8	11	13	15	17	18	20								
NSC: 1965–67	5	7	11	13	14	16	18	20	21	23	25	26	27	31	32	
FGS: 1968–70	7	10	11	13	15	17										
NSC: 1968–69	7	11	14	17	19	22	23	27	28	29	31	33	33			
White Children																
FGS: 1965–67	4	7	9	11	13	15	19	18								
NSC: 1965–67	4	6	9	11	13	15	16	17	18	20	21	21	22	24	27	29
FGS: 1968–70	5	8	10	13	14											
NSC: 1968–69	5	10	13	16	18	20	22	24	25	26	28	29	30			
Black Children																
FGS: 1965–67	16	18	24	26	29	33	35	37								
NSC: 1965–67	12	16	18	20	20	21	23	25	26	27	29	36	36	37	41	41
FGS: 1968–70	23	29	33	37	42											
NSC: 1968–69	20	20	22	28	29	33	33	47	48	50	50	51	51			

[1] Proportion based on children born after their mother's first marriage and currently living with at least one biological parent.

Based on data from F.F. Furstenberg, J.L. Peterson, C.W. Nord & N. Zill (1983). The life course of children of divorce: Marital disruption and parental contact, *American Sociological Review*, **48**, 656–668.

data in Table 2.2. Most children who experience a divorce experience it in their early childhood years. For example, of the children in the 1968–69 NSC cohort, 22% had experienced a parental divorce by age six. To put it another way, two-thirds of the children who would experience divorce by age 12, had already experienced it by age six. Infants are even more likely to experience a divorce than are preschoolers. Data from the Family Growth Survey indicate that of all children experiencing a divorce by age six, 40% did so in their first year of life, 20% between ages one and two, 15% between ages two and three, 10% between ages three and four, and 15% between ages four and five (Bumpass & Rindfuss, 1979).

Children's Postdivorce Living Arrangements

Where do children live after a divorce? Despite popular views which depict an increasing rate of paternal custody, about 10 times as many children reside with a single mother as a single father (SCCYF, 1983), and that proportion does not appear to be changing (Emery, Hetherington, & DiLalla, 1984). Two factors related to the frequency with which children reside with their father are their age and sex. According to the 1983 census data, 1.5% boys under the age three lived with their father and 3.6% boys aged 15 to 17 did so. The comparable figures for girls were 1.3% under age three and 2.6% aged 15 to 17 (U.S. Bureau of the Census, 1984). In contrast, age and sex are generally unrelated to mother custody. For the same census data the following percentages were obtained: 19.6% boys under age 3; 20.6% boys 15 to 17; 19.5% girls under age 3; and 19.4% girls 15 to 17 (U.S. Bureau of the Census, 1984). Thus, older children, particularly older boys, are more likely to live with their fathers than are younger ones.

Remarriage also influences living arrangements. According to the data in Table 2.1, 10% of all children lived with a biological parent and a stepparent in 1982. While the census data on remarriage are not reported separately for black and white children, evidence from the NSC indicates that within five years following a marital disruption, four of seven white children enter into stepfamilies compared to one of eight black children. Cohort influences also seem to be important to remarriage experiences. Bumpass (1984a) has estimated that the lower rate of remarriage during the 1970s means that children will enter stepfamilies less rapidly. According to his data, only 35% white children and 12% black children born after 1970 entered a stepfamily within five years following their parents' divorce.

The higher divorce rate for second marriages, projected to be about 60% (Glick, 1984), has one more important influence on children. Of the children in the NSC sample who had one parent who remarried, 37.3% experienced a second divorce (Furstenberg et al.,

1983). As noted earlier, while the presence of biological children appears to be a disincentive to divorce in first marriages, the presence of stepchildren is related to an increased likelihood of divorce in remarriage.

SUMMARY

Anthropological, historical, and demographic findings make it clear that the concept of family and the consequences of divorce vary across time, culture, and subculture. This conclusion is important to consider in the abstract sense of recognizing the limits of our knowledge. Many of our cultural beliefs and much of our scientific information about child-rearing, the family, and divorce are bound by culture and time. This conclusion is also important in helping us examine cultural stereotypes. The diversity of children's divorce experiences suggests that each of us as individuals be cautious in extrapolating from our own experiences to those of others. We must be particularly cautious about labeling divorce or single parenthood as inevitably "bad," lest we similarly label those segments of our society in which these are becoming the modal family structures.

This concern with negative stereotypes is not intended as a suggestion that divorce is somehow an innocuous event that would cause few difficulties if we only thought about it differently. The weight of clinical and research evidence, as discussed in later chapters, suggests that divorce is an exceedingly difficult transition for many children and their parents. What factors make the transition difficult, how children respond to them, and how these families in transition can be helped are topics that are addressed in subsequent chapters.

By thinking about these issues not only from the individual perspective of psychology, but also from some of the broad perspectives presented in this chapter, creativity is encouraged in understanding and intervening with children and families. Indeed, the suggestion that there are cultures in which divorce has a less adverse impact on children is an optimistic view, which implies that if some of the processes divorce entails can be altered, then some of its negative consequences for children can be avoided.

Before thoroughly examining the current state of our knowledge of the effects of divorce on children, let us pause to carefully consider the research methods involved.

3

METHODOLOGICAL AND CONCEPTUAL ISSUES IN DIVORCE RESEARCH

Given its complexity and social relevance, research on children and divorce must be interpreted with an awareness of its limitations. Hence, some central methodological and conceptual issues are discussed in this chapter. Among the topics considered are methodological limitations associated with different sampling and measurement procedures, alternative causal explanations inherent in correlational research, and the unavoidable confounding of children's age at divorce, time since divorce, and current age.

METHODOLOGICAL ISSUES

Many methodological issues in divorce research apply to studies of family or child development in general, and a thorough review of such a broad topic is well beyond the scope of this chapter. The present overview therefore is limited to a brief discussion of two basic issues as they pertain to research on divorce and children: sampling and measurement.

Sampling

Representative samples. The major sampling concern in divorce research is one that has been of great concern to sociologists, but is often not carefully addressed by psychologists, namely, whether the sample is representative of a larger population to which findings can be generalized (Furstenberg, 1985). While sampling is largely irrelevant in some areas of psychological investigation, divorce is not one of them.

Research on social issues such as divorce is often used to draw inferences about broader groups than those included in the study, and findings can quickly be translated into suggestions for social policy. Because of this, it is critical that sampling limitations be recognized and that some studies of representative samples be conducted. Unfortunately, many researchers, and consumers of research, have made the obvious mistake of generalizing from small, unrepresentative samples to the entire population of children whose parents have or will divorce.

A particular problem encountered in unrepresentative sampling is the use of studies of clinic samples for drawing conclusions about the nonclinic population. This is not just a problem conceptually; research has also shown a number of empirical differences in the process, outcome, and predictors of adjustment in clinic and nonclinic samples (Emery, 1982; Emery & O'Leary, 1984; O'Leary & Emery, 1984). Inappropriate generalizations across ethnic groups is another particular problem (Cherlin, 1981; Peters & McAdoo, 1983). As emphasized in Chapter 2, a number of racial and socio-economic factors are associated with family status, and different social supports for divorced families have evolved in various subcultures. Research on divorce in a white, middle-class sample may be irrelevant to the experience of different ethnic or socio-economic groups.

Cohort effects. A second sampling issue in divorce research, cohort effects, raises questions about the accuracy of generalizing across time, rather than across groups. A cohort is a group of people who experience a common event within a given period of time, with this event forming the basis for group membership. Year of birth is often used to define cohort membership. For example, everyone born between 1920 and 1929 might be considered to be part of the cohort reared during the Depression.

Although they are rarely studied, cohort effects may be important for research on divorce. For instance, it is possible that the experience of a parental divorce was quite different for children reared in the 1950s than for children reared in the 1970s. Divorce was less common and less socially acceptable during the earlier period, and parents who divorced then probably had more compelling reasons to do so than parents who divorced in the 1970s. Children from more recent birth cohorts may thus have experienced less adverse family environments both before and after divorce than did children from earlier cohorts. In addition, divorced children who grew up in the 1970s were probably less likely to be considered as being "different" by their peers. This raises the ironic possibility that the increased prevalence of divorce in the last two decades may have helped to facilitate children's social and psychological adjustment to it.

It is conceivable that rapidly changing divorce laws may have differentially influenced even very recent birth cohorts. Depending on the year of divorce and the state of residence, one study conducted in the 1970s may include families who obtained a fault divorce, knew that the court preferred maternal custody, or reached a settlement in an adversarial hearing. A second study, in contrast, might include families who obtained a no-fault divorce, who were pushed toward joint custody, or who reached a settlement in mandatory mediation. (See Chapter 7 for a discussion of legal issues in contemporary divorces.) Consideration of cohort effects harkens back to a point made earlier, namely, that broad social influences impact on children's adjustment to divorce. These influences have changed rapidly in recent years, making cohort effects not only possible but plausible.

Self-selection to divorce. The fact that a divorce is not equally likely to occur among an entire population of families is another sampling issue that merits attention. Families "self-select" to divorce, and to the extent that divorced parents differ from married parents, their children potentially differ from children in married families in ways other than the experience of divorce. Parental personality characteristics, predivorce family interaction patterns, and even genetic factors may predispose parents both to divorce and to produce children with particular types of personalities.

An example of self-selection is the finding that divorce occurs more often when one spouse suffers from a severe psychiatric disorder (Emery, Weintraub, & Neale, 1982). While it is certainly not true that every person who divorces is emotionally disturbed, children who have a mentally disordered parent may be oversampled in some studies of divorce. The issue is complicated further because one researcher has found evidence for an interactive effect between divorce and parental antisocial personality disorder (Rutter, 1971), while another research group has found that marital conflict accounted for the relation between psychiatric status and children's adjustment problems in school for affectively disordered but not for schizophrenic parents (Emery et al., 1982).

While the parental psychopathology issue may be relevant to some studies, particularly those that employ clinic samples, much more important is the general point that divorced parents, and therefore their children, may differ from the larger population of families in variables that are unknown and perhaps unknowable. This concern is actually a special case of the third variable problem, discussed below. Parents who divorce may differ from parents who do not divorce on unmeasured third variables, and these may account for any differences found in their children's psychological functioning. As with other third-variable problems, the best solution is the measurement and statistical control of theoretically relevant constructs, particularly in conjunction with longitudinal research designs.

Base rates. Unrepresentative samples, cohort effects, and subject self-selection—all three can potentially limit the generality of findings. The last sampling issue discussed here, the base rate problem, imposes a different type of limitation. When the base rate of a predictor variable (divorce in this case) differs from that of the variable to be predicted (various measures of child adjustment), there are statistical limitations regarding the extent to which the two measures can be associated (Meehl & Rosen, 1955).

The base rate problem is best illustrated with an example (see Table 3.1). Assume that in a hypothetical follow-back study a very

TABLE 3.1
Illustration of the Base Rate Problem in a Hypothetical Study
Predicting Delinquency from Divorced Family Status

	Criterion Variable	
	Delinquent	Not Delinquent
Divorced	80	320 400
	(true positive)	(false positive)
Predictor Variable		
Not Divorced	20	580 600
	(false negative)	(true negative)
	100	900 1000

Data in this table reflect the assumptions that in this hypothetical follow-up study: 4 outof 10 children come from divorced families; 1 out of 10 childrenbecome delinquent; and 8 out of 10 delinquents come from divorced homes. The high rate of false positives when predicting delinquency from divorce illustrates that differing base rates can impede prediction, even given an apparently strong association between predictor and criterion variables.

strong association between deliquency and divorce is found. When delinquents are sampled and their family experience is examined retrospectively, 8 out of every 10 are found to come from divorced families. Assume further that, because of this strong association, divorce is now used as a prospective predictor of delinquency in a second hypothetical study, a follow-up of children not known to be delinquent currently. Assume that the follow-back study is perfectly replicated in the second investigation, i.e., 8 out of every 10 children who become delinquent are found once again to be from divorced families. Does this mean that divorce was a good predictor of delinquency in the follow-up study? This is where population base rates become important.

Assume that the base rate of parental divorce was 40% in the follow-up sample, and the base rate of delinquency was 10%. As can be seen in Table 3.1, when these base rates are assumed, divorce proves to be a poor prospective predictor of delinquency, yielding a false positive rate of 80%. Using divorce as an indicator, 400 children would be pedicted to become delinquent, but 320 of them would *not* be adjudicated as minors. (The false negative rate (3%) is much better given the present assumptions, but it, too, could be distorted markedly by changing the base rates.) A quick glance at Table 3.1 reveals that the assumptions about base rates and the link between divorce and delinquency have been met. Moreover, the problem cannot be one of chance error given the high degree of validity and perfect cross-validation that were assumed. Rather, the problem stems from a basic statistical limitation. False positive and false negative rates are not merely a function of the strength of association; they also depend upon the base rates of the predictor and criterion variables (Meehl & Rosen, 1955). In general, this means that, for statistical reasons alone, divorce cannot be an efficient predictor of variables which have much higher or lower base rates. Given the high base rate of divorce and the low base rate of many variables one wishes to predict (e.g., various indicators of child adjustment problems), the base rate issue can be a serious problem in divorce research.

Measurement

The adequacy of measurement is another basic methodological issue that is essential to consider in divorce research. Having recently reviewed measurement concerns elsewhere (Emery, Joyce, & Fincham, 1987), only two basic points will be made here. First, sound measurement, the hallmark of psychological research, is particularly weak in the two areas most relevant to the present topic: assessing children's psychological functioning (other than their intellectual capacity and academic performance) and evaluating the quality of family relationships. Weaknesses in each area include conceptual and empirical limitations. There is continuing controversy about the major constructs of both children's mental health and family relationships, and there are few operational measures of existing constructs in either domain that meet accepted psychometric standards for reliability and validity (Emery et al., 1987). Perhaps the biggest potential problem stemming from these measurement inadequacies is that the *failure* to find predicted differences may be caused partially or solely by unreliable or invalid measurement. While the samples obtained are often carefully selected, survey research is notably weak in terms of the psychometrics of the measures employed. Thus, null findings from a survey study must be viewed with particular caution.

A second measurement problem that has plagued research on marriage, children, and divorce is that raters who provide evaluations of one area typically are not "blind" to the status of the other domain. For example, a mother might rate both the extent of conflict with her child's father and the degree to which her son disobeys her. Similarly, a teacher may be asked to evaluate a child who is known to come from a "broken home." Bias can obviously distort such ratings, perhaps in different directions, depending on the rater and the experimental demands.

Because the best evaluations of children are likely to come from those who are aware of their family circumstances, it may be impossible to circumvent the response-bias problem completely. One way to minimize this problem is to use multiple informants, so that systematic individual biases will not be unduly influential. Another solution is to develop instruments which quantify bias in parents', teachers', and children's reports, which has been done with some self-report instruments designed for adults, such as the MMPI lie scales. Measures of response bias could be used to correct substantive ratings and may be of considerable interest in their own right. Finally, sound observational measures of both parental and child behavior are also valuable in dealing with self-report bias, but problems in sampling the interactions of interest and in coding subtle aspects of family interaction limit the general use of this alternative (Emery et al., 1987).

INTERPRETING CORRELATIONS BETWEEN
MARITAL AND CHILD PROBLEMS

Even if perfect measurement of a perfect sample was possible, any association found between divorce and children's adjustment would present interpretive difficulties. This is obviously true because such research is necessarily correlational in design. One can hardly assign children to experience a parental divorce at random. As gratuitous as this observation may sound, assumptions of causality are difficult to avoid. Many comparisons between divorced children and a "control group" of married children have attributed the differences obtained between the two groups to divorce. This causal conclusion may be accurate, but third-variable and reverse-causality considerations promote conceptual clarity and raise plausible, often important, alternative interpretations.

Causal Direction

Unlike what children themselves sometimes believe, no one has suggested that children are responsible for their parents' divorce. As mentioned in Chapter 2, however, children do exert some important influences on divorce, which have been duly documented. Demographic data indicate that the presence of children may inhibit, increase, or have no apparent influence on the likelihood of divorce, depending upon a number of conditions. While not ubiquitous, the deterrent effect, historically at least, has been the most robust. It is the rare parent who has not agonized over how his or her children will be affected by a divorce, and many partners *are* staying together for their children's sake.

The presence of children not only influences the likelihood of divorce, but also has an effect on marital satisfaction. On average, the effect is negative (Glenn & McLanahan, 1981, 1982). This conclusion is based on comparisons of the reported marital satisfaction of large samples of couples with and without children, and the finding is bolstered by various smaller-scale investigations of the transition to parenthood. Research in this latter vein indicates that the birth of the first child has a negative mean impact on marital satisfaction (Belsky & Isabella, 1985; Waldron & Routh, 1981).

Both these findings are consistent with a third line of research in which a U-shaped relation between marital satisfaction and the stage in the family life cycle has been reported. Although it accounts for a relatively small proportion of the variance, some researchers have found that marital satisfaction is highest during the first few years of marriage before children are born, it declines and remains below earlier peaks while children are in their preschool and school-age years, and rises again as the children become teenagers and young adults and the nest begins to empty (Anderson, Russell, & Schumm, 1983).

A paradox is encountered in attempting to reconcile the literature on children's impact on marital dissolution with children's influence on marital satisfaction. How can the presence of children be associated with *more* marital distress but a *lower* divorce rate? While children apparently decrease the benefits of marriage, they more than offset this by increasing the costs associated with divorce. Indeed, it has been suggested that the relation between the presence of children and marital distress is explained by the fact that children deter unhappily married couples from divorcing (Glenn & McLanahan, 1982).

Research on how children influence divorce and marital satisfaction is of obvious importance in its own right. This line of research is of equal or greater value from a general conceptual perspective, however. One important consideration stemming from this reverse-causality perspective is that divorces involving children are likely to differ from childless divorces. Indeed, in many states the procedures for obtaining a divorce are different for couples with and without children. For example, some states require a longer waiting period for a no-fault divorce when minor children are involved (Freed & Foster, 1981). Other important, but undocumented, differences may also exist. For example, partners with children may work harder to find acceptable compromises in their marriage, but one consequence of this may be that severe conflicts and trial separations are more common.

Probably the most important consequence of reverse-causality considerations is that the recognition of reciprocal influence directs conceptualization toward a systems-oriented view of the family process (Minuchin, 1985). Parents influence children, children influence parents, and the relationships between various family members influence those outside, as well as those inside, the subsystem. Families are organized according to explicit or implicit hierarchies which, except in troubled circumstances, give parents power over minor children. Legitimized authority is not the only means of influencing others, however. In addition to the global influences outlined above, parents and marriages are affected by their children in many subtle ways. To give one clinical example, some parents may deny or avoid their marital conflict by using a child as a scapegoat, blaming him for the family's difficulties. Presumably blaming the child strengthens the parental alliance, and thus the scapegoated child "improves" the marriage. Recognition of such patterns of mutual influence does not readily follow from a pure "adult effects" model of child development.

Third Variables

While consideration of reverse causality raises some important substantive and conceptual points, no one has suggested that divorce is correlated with child behavior problems only because the presence of troubled children causes divorce. The idea that the relation between divorce and children's adjustment problems can be fully accounted for by certain third variables is plausible, however. Third-variable explanations not only offer compelling conceptual alternatives, but suggest substantive directions for refocusing research and intervention (Blechman, 1982).

The significance of third variables becomes apparent when some of the most relevant alternatives are considered. Various investigators have suggested that the passage of time (Hetherington, 1979), interparental conflict (Emery, 1982), child-rearing practices (Hess & Camara, 1979), parental mental health (Wallerstein & Kelly, 1980), or low income (Herzog & Sudia, 1973) explain a greater proportion of the variance in the correlation between divorce and child behavior problems than does the event of divorce. While these various family changes often *are* consequences of divorce, the point, both conceptually and practically, is to avoid the mistake of attributing the outcomes to divorce per se rather than to the series of events—the third variables—associated with it. Indeed, these third variables are of sufficient substantive importance to be the entire focus of Chapter 5. At present, it suffices to raise a few general, conceptual issues.

First, it is essential that various theoretically relevant third variables be measured in studies of divorce and children. Factors such as the amount of time since the separation or divorce, the type of custody arrangement, the amount of parent-child contact, and the family's economic standing are potentially important predictors of children's postdivorce adjustment. Other variables such as the quality of the affection in parent-child relationships, discipline practices, and parental conflict may be significant correlates of child adjustment in one- *and* two-parent families. While the list of possible third variables is endless and sample size limits the number that can be considered simultaneously in any single study, divorce researchers increasingly need to compare their relative predictive power.

A final point to be made about third variables is that they highlight the need for longitudinal research. Examination of the timing of the onset of these correlated events in relation to each other and to changes in children's psychological states can help to untangle causal issues that cannot be addressed in cross-sectional designs. There have been a few longitudinal studies of children and families who were recruited soon after a divorce, and the findings from these investigations substantiate the value of prospective research. Furthermore, because many relevant changes in family relationships may begin before divorce occurs, it is essential that measurement in some longitudinal studies begin when both parents are still residing together in the family home. As discussed in Chapter 5, the high rate of divorce has made it possible to use some investigations of normal child development as prospective studies of divorce, but more work is required. Because of its importance, this chapter closes with a discussion of some specific issues in longitudinal research.

LONGITUDINAL RESEARCH AND TEMPORAL INFLUENCES ON CHILDREN'S DIVORCE ADJUSTMENT

Most research on children and divorce has been cross-sectional in design; in other words, children have been assessed at only one point in time. There are obvious practical advantages to this strategy, but findings from cross-sectional research can be difficult to interpret. As noted above, causal inference is limited. However, the present concern is that three theoretically relevant variables, all of which are related to the passage of time, are confounded in research on children and divorce. The three intertwined temporal variables are: (1) the age of the child at the time of separation or divorce, (2) the child's current age, and (3) the length of time that has lapsed since the separation or divorce. (Historical period, as discussed earlier in the chapter, is a fourth potential temporal confound, but its more subtle influence is not considered here.)

To illustrate the confounding of the three temporal variables, consider the frequent assertion that divorce is more detrimental to children when it occurs before they reach five or six years of age. This assertion assumed that a researcher has found in assessing children at age 13, that those who were four years old when their parents divorced have more problems in school than those who were eight years old at the time of divorce.

This evidence would be consistent with the early divorce hypothesis. However, it is also consistent with the hypothesis that the longer children live in a single-parent family, the more academic difficulties they develop. In fact, in any cross-sectional study in which early-divorce and late-divorce groups of same-age children are compared, the time that has passed since divorce will be a plausible alternative explanation. In all such studies, age at the time of divorce will correlate perfectly with the time that has elapsed since the divorce. That this is true can be readily demonstrated, as shown in Figure 3.1 (see section labeled "Cross-Sectional Study 1"). If the children of divorced parents are all assessed at age 13 (or any other age), and we know what their age was when their parents divorced, we can precisely determine the time lapse since the divorce. In this example, it is five years for the age eight divorce cohort, and nine years for the age four divorce cohort.

The confounding of these three temporal variables can be illustrated more dramatically with another hypothetical example of cross-sectional research. Assume that a researcher wants to compare a group of children whose parents divorced when they were four years old with a group whose parents divorced when they were eight years old, but the researcher thinks it essential to hold time since divorce constant. In order to do this, the two groups would have to be equated not on chronological age but on the amount of time that has passed since the divorce. If the time since divorce is set at three years, the result would be a comparison of "equivalent" groups of seven-year-olds and eleven-year-olds. This design is also illustrated in Figure 3.1 (see section labeled "Cross-Sectional Study 2"). Obviously, developmental researchers are reluctant to suggest that children of different ages are equivalent. For some good reasons, however, many researchers are also reluctant to say that two groups of divorced children are equivalent if they differ in terms of age at separation or

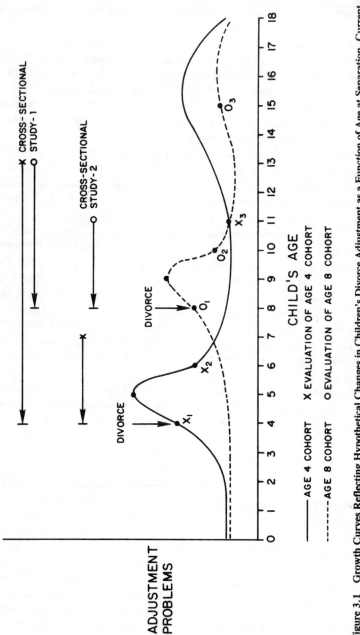

Figure 3.1 Growth Curves Reflecting Hypothetical Changes in Children's Divorce Adjustment as a Function of Age at Separation, Current Age, and Time Since Separation

divorce or time that has passed since separation or divorce. But we have just seen that these variables are inextricably confounded.

Formally, the issue at hand is an age-cohort-period problem. Any two of these three temporal variables perfectly define the third (Baltes, Cornelius, & Nesselroade, 1979). To give a more straightforward example of an age-cohort-period problem, for a birth cohort in which membership is defined as being born in 1952 and age known to be 35 years, the historical period is perfectly determined—1987. In this context, the problem is obvious. Given information about any two of the following—(1) year of birth, (2) age, or (3) current year—the third can be readily determined.

The logic of the age-cohort-period problem is a bit more complicated in the present example, because the child's age at the time of divorce defines the cohort membership, the time since the divorce is the equivalent of age, and current age is analogous to the historical period. Terminology aside, the point is that the three temporal variables must be confounded in divorce research, as they are in all age-cohort-period problems.

There is no accepted solution for untangling the independent effects of age, cohort, and period, even in longitudinal research designs (Baltes et al., 1979). To illustrate some potential problems that might be encountered consider the hypothetical growth curves presented in Figure 3.1 (for discussion of the use of growth curves in developmental research, see McArdle & Epstein, 1987). These curves reflect changes in children's divorce adjustment as a function of the three temporal variables under discussion. Specifically, they reflect the hypothetical assumptions that: (1) divorce is more harmful when children are younger at the time of divorce, (2) children's adjustment problems initially increase then improve over time, and (3) adolesence is a particularly difficult time for children from divorced families. These are all reasonable assumptions reflecting cohort (age at separation), age (time since separation), and period (current age) effects respectively. The growth curves associated with them are also straightforward but, as illustrated in Figure 3.1, potential problems in longitudinal research can be easily detected.

In the ambitious (and hypothetical) longitudinal study portrayed in the Figure, the two cohorts of children would be assessed at the time of divorce, two years later, and five years after that (X_1, X_2, and X_3 denote assessements of the Age 4 cohort, while O_1, O_2, and O_3 denote assessments of the Age 8 cohort.) From this study one may correctly conclude that children's divorce adjustment improved over time, but the deterioration during the first year after divorce and the particularly stressful nature of adolescent transition would not be detected. Furthermore, it would be incorrect to suggest that divorce is initially more trying for members of the "early divorce" group, but over time they adjust as well as members of the "late divorce" cohort.

The issues could be complicated further by adding considerations of variables such as changes in family life during the time since divorce (e.g., remarriage). Such a series of suggestions would become immobilizing, however. Rather than beating such a retreat, because of the age-cohort-period problem, children's age simply is not considered as an individual difference variable in the discussion of cross-sectional research on children's adjustment presented in Chapter 4. Substantive findings related to the three temporal issues are raised again in Chapter 5. Although no firm resolution to the problem exists, empirical construction of growth curves such as the hypothetical ones displayed in Figure 3.1 is a fresh approach to this tricky problem (McArdle & Epstein, 1987), albeit one with substantial demands for data collection.

SUMMARY

Several cautions have been raised in this chapter concerning the methodology and interpretation of research on marriage, children, and divorce. A brief glance at the chapter sub-headings reveals that the issues discussed are basic to social science research. Unrepresentative sampling, insufficiently reliable measurement, problems in inferring causation from correlation, and complexities in longitudinal designs are hardly unique to divorce research.

On the one hand, the litany of research problems appears discouraging, and a reasonable reaction to them might be to disregard any study that does not meet some very high standard of research quality and examine only the very small pool of "adequate" studies. On the other hand, however, methodological and interpretive differences between studies can be viewed as pieces of a puzzle which, if solved, can be constructed into a picture that is more complete than any that could be provided by a single, but impossible, "perfect" study. Like the seven blind men who felt different parts of an elephant, various investigations are limited in that only narrow aspects of the divorce process were considered. But not every researcher needs to study the whole elephant. Just as the tail or the trunk is a part of the elephant, the study of a narrow sample or a narrow problem is a part of the total picture of divorce. The key is to be able to remove the blindfold in order to identify the strengths and limitations of each study. Otherwise it might be mistakenly concluded that the trunk *is* the elephant.

In the following chapters a wide variety of studies are pieced together in an attempt to construct a relatively complete picture of children's experiences of the divorce process. Hopefully, this has been done with an awareness of the limitations of existing research.

4

CROSS-SECTIONAL RESEARCH ON THE ADJUSTMENT OF CHILDREN OF DIVORCE

Although divorce is best conceptualized as a process of change which extends over time and across a number of areas of family functioning, in this chapter divorce is treated as if it were a unitary event that is, or is not, associated with certain outcomes among children. While generalizations from this cross-sectional approach necessarily obscure individual differences both in family process and in children's accommodation of change, they provide a snapshot that is helpful in several ways.

In certain respects, a discussion of the outcomes of divorce is of interest in its own right. The social category, "divorce," is hardly homogeneous in terms of the economic, social, or psychological experiences of the individuals it groups together. Still, as with other socio-legal classifications, generalizations about its average effects are quite useful. While some interventions, like psychotherapy, are appropriately concerned with individual families, broad-scale policies are necessarily designed for the "typical" family. For such purposes, global conclusions about divorce can be of value, although one must be mindful that diversity is intentionally ignored.

A cross-sectional picture also facilitates an understanding of the process. It is necessary to document at least some differences in the outcome, if only to provide justification for research which focuses on developmental processes. Broadly stated, epidemiological analysis can help to specify some of the conditions under which relations of interest must hold. Theoretical explanations regarding the mechanisms of effect must be congruent with cross-sectional findings. For example, as shown in this chapter, evidence indicates that there is *not* a one-to-one relation between divorce and psychological problems among children. More-over, divorce is associated with more adverse outcomes than is parental death, and children function better in conflict-free divorced families than in conflict-ridden two-parent families (Emery, 1982). Such findings specify a relation between divorce and children's adjustment which contravenes theories that focus solely on the developmental importance of family structure.

With these cautions and benefits in mind, cross-sectional evidence on the psychological outcomes of divorce for children is reviewed below. Seven specific areas of functioning are examined: (1) utilization of mental health services; (2) externalizing problems, such as delinquency, aggression, and disobedience; (3) internalizing problems, including depression, anxiety, and low self-esteem; (4) intellectual and academic functioning; (5) gender-role and heterosexual behavior; (6) prosocial skills; and (7) functioning during adult life. In reviewing the various studies the moderating influences of sex, race, and socio-economic status are noted when data are available. Temporal influences, including children's age, and family processes are the foci of the next chapter, where individual differences are discussed in an attempt to turn the snapshots presented here into a moving picture.

UTILIZATION OF MENTAL HEALTH SERVICES

Research on the relation between parental divorce and the utilization of mental health services is important for at least two broad reasons. First, use of such services is an important indicator in its own right, as clinicians have observed that children from divorced families are over-represented in outpatient mental health clinics (Kalter, 1977; Kalter & Rembar, 1981; Tuckman & Regan, 1966). Second, many studies of divorce have focused on clinic-referred children, but there are a number of problems in generalizing from such samples. Clinic-referred children may be self-selected on variables that cannot be readily identified (Emery, Binkoff, Houts, & Carr, 1983). In addition to problematic child behavior, factors such as parental guilt, expectancy bias, or the stress of single parenting may increase the likelihood of referral.

Because of the problems in generalizing from clinic samples, it is essential that nonclinic groups be studied. Unfortunately, most studies of nonclinic samples are also limited, either because they were com-posed of narrow demographic groups, the families were recruited in such a way that it is not possible to draw inferences about the population they represent, and/or the demographic characteristics of the samples were not considered or reported.

Fortunately, a handful of researchers have conducted studies of large and diverse samples of children. The most impressive of these is the National Survey of Children (NSC), an investigation of a nationally representative sample of 2,258 children aged seven to eleven years who were first assessed in 1976. Eighty percent of the families contacted in this stratified probability sample agreed to participate, and information on family functioning and the children's adjustment was gathered from children (a maximum of two per family), mothers (in 95% of the cases), and schools (for 1,682 children) (Zill, 1978).

Various findings from the NSC are presented at different points throughout this book. Among the most important is that, in a sample of families representative of the population of the United States, children of divorce were found to be more likely to consult a mental health professional. Of the parents in the NSC sample who had divorced, 14% believed that their children had experienced problems in the past year that were serious enough to warrant some sort of professional help. Thirteen percent of the children from divorced households had actually seen a psychologist or a psychiatrist at some point in time. In contrast, among children living with their two biological parents, 6.0% were identified by their mothers as having had problems serious enough to require professional help, and 5.5% had actually seen a mental health professional (Zill, 1978).

These figures must be interpreted with some caution because mental health contacts, as well as the mothers' views on the need for professional help, are potentially biased indicators. However, Zill (1978) also found that *teachers* rated children from separated and divorced families as engaging in significantly more aggressive behavior than children whose parents had "very happy" marriages. Children whose parents had "fairly happy" marriages, in turn, were rated as being more aggressive than children from "very happy" marriages. (Marital satisfaction was determined by mothers' response to a single structured item. The "very happy" group included 69% of the married parents in the sample; 28.5% reported being "fairly happy," and 2.5% said they were "not too happy.")

In addition to the teacher reports, significantly more *children* from separated and divorced families reported that they had gotten into a fight in school in the past week, compared to children whose parents had "very happy" marriages. On this measure, children living with parents who were "not too happy" in their marriage had even more fights than children whose parents were divorced.

Cross-sectional studies, such as the NSC, are limited in that they cannot capture the experiences of children as they proceed through the divorce transition, and pragmatics constrain the depth of measurement in a sample of this size. Nevertheless, the NSC data indicate that, in a nationally representative sample, children whose parents have divorced are at an increased risk for experiencing psychological difficulties as indexed by mental-health utilization rates and independent parent, teacher, and child reports. This is true even when socio-economic factors are controlled (Zill, 1978). Given similar findings in epidemiological studies in other English-speaking countries (Ferguson, Dimond, & Horwood, 1986; Wadsworth, Burnell, Taylor, & Butler, 1985), it can be concluded that the general population of children whose parents have divorced have more adjustment problems, on the average, than do children whose parents are happily married. Among children aged seven to eleven years living in the United States, a parental divorce is associated with a two to three times greater likelihood of contact with a mental-health professional (Zill, 1978).

While this is an extremely important conclusion, another aspect of the NSC data may be of even greater significance. If only 13% of children of divorced parents consult a mental-health professional, then over 85% children aged seven to eleven cope without professional help. This much more optimistic view of the NSC data does not mean that the divorce transition was painless for these children, or that painful memories about the divorce no longer linger. The frequency of pathological outcomes of divorce should not be overstated, but neither should the difficulties involved in the process of change be underestimated.

Having made these points about global adjustment, more specific behavioral outcomes are examined below.

EXTERNALIZING PROBLEMS

The observation that youths from single-parent families were overrepresented among delinquents served as an early and influential impetus for concern that divorce causes externalizing problems among children (e.g., Glueck & Glueck, 1950). In the 1950s and early 1960s, a number of studies were published on delinquency and single mothers. Because psychoanalytic and social learning theories suggest that fathers play a central role in the moral development (and sex typing) of their sons, much of this research focused on the effects of "father absence" on boys. Given this focus, children who were not living with their fathers because of divorce, death, or out-of-wedlock birth were considered by some theorists to be a homogeneous group. Indeed, Herzog and Sudia (1973) noted that some commentators expanded the group to include children whose fathers had recurring sea duty as a part of their naval service!

While father-absence research was widely accepted, even one of the most influential and most highly criticized studies of father absence, conducted by Sheldon and Eleanor Glueck (1950), did not focus exclusively on family structure. In comparing delinquent boys with a matched nondelinquent group, 61% of the delinquent and 34% of the nondelinquent youth were found to come from single-mother families. While this difference was statistically significant, father absence was ranked only 15th out of 41 family factors studied as potential discriminators between groups, and it was not included among the five social indicators in the Gluecks' (unsuccessful) prediction tables. Rather, the social prediction index comprised measures of paternal discipline, maternal supervision, paternal affection, maternal affection, and family cohesion (Glueck & Glueck, 1950).

Despite some early attempts to focus on family process rather than family structure (e.g., McCord, McCord, & Thurber, 1962; Nye, 1957), "father absent" has only recently been widely recognized as an inappropriate psychological category (Levitin, 1979). While it now seems clear that factors such as interparental conflict largely account for the outcome (Emery, 1982), the basic observation made by early delinquency and divorce researchers still has some validity. Divorce has consistently been found to be associated with externalizing problems among children. There is little need to review the research that substantiates this conclusion in detail because the association has been so well documented. To cite some of the more prominent examples: Children whose parents were divorced were judged to be more aggressive according to mothers,' teachers,' and their own reports in the initial NSC survey (Zill, 1978), as well as the five-year follow-up (Peterson & Zill, 1986). Rutter (1971) reported similar findings in his epidemiological study of British children, and increased antisocial behavior was also found among five-year-olds living in one-parent families in a national evaluation of 12,743 British families (Wadsworth et al., 1985). In their intensive, multimethod study of a nonclinic sample of four- to six-year-olds, Hetherington, Cox, and Cox (1978) found children whose parents were divorced to be more disobedient, aggressive, demanding, and lacking in self-control. Numerous investigators who have evaluated clinic-referred children from divorced families have found a higher frequency of conduct problems among them than among clinic-referred children from two-parent families (McDermott, 1968, 1970; Tuckman & Regan, 1966). Children whose parents have been divorced *are* over-represented among delinquents according to the self-reports of boys (Goldstein, 1984) and girls (Kalter, Riemer, Brickman, & Chen, 1985), as well as official delinquency statistics (Wadsworth, 1979). Finally, several reviewers have agreed that greater levels of aggression are found among children whose parents are divorced, particularly among boys (e.g., Emery, 1982; Emery et al., 1984; Felner, Farber, & Primavera, 1980; Lamb, 1977).

Despite the impressive convergence of evidence, several points require clarification. First, it must be noted that family status is linked to two other important social correlates of delinquency, namely, race and socio-economic status. The independent contributions of these three confounded variables in explaining delinquency rates still have not been untangled (Rutter & Giller, 1983). Second, many adolescents who violate the law are not adjudicated; thus, delinquency statistics reflect both the youth's behavior and decisions made by legal professionals. While family status is related to self-reported as well as official delinquency, the stability of a child's family is one factor frequently considered in decisions about whether to arrest and prosecute youth or not (Farrington, 1979). Third, it is certainly not true that every child whose parents divorce becomes a juvenile delinquent. Because of differing population base rates, delinquency predicts family status much better than family status predicts delinquency (Meehl & Rosen, 1955; see also Chapter 3). Moreover, most externalizing problems that accompany divorce are far less serious than violations of the law. Fourth, externalizing problems are caused by many, as yet unspecified, factors. Contemporary divorce researchers recognize that they are documenting information more relevant to understanding the consequences of divorce than the etiology of aggression. Fifth, since certain subtypes of externalizing problems are likely to have different etiological pathways, one may expect them to be differentially associated with divorce and its correlates. For example, since hyperactivity is commonly assumed to be of somatogenic origin, no relation between it and divorce can be expected. In fact, marital conflict was found to be unrelated to hyperactivity in one investigation (Prinz, de Meyers, Holden, Tarnowski, & Roberts, 1983), although such conflict did distinguish hyperactives from a comparison group in a second study (Befera & Barkley, 1985). Finally, given that it is not father absence alone that is linked with externalizing problems among children whose parents have divorced, there is considerable controversy over which factors might account for the increased conduct disorders. As discussed further in Chapter 5, involvement in parental conflict, lowered family income, and altered disciplinary practices are some of the most commonly considered influences.

INTERNALIZING PROBLEMS

While the increased prevalence of externalizing problems is well established, findings with regard to internalizing problems are much more equivocal. This, to say the least, is somewhat surprising, since several theoretical perspectives, most notably psychoanalytic views, suggest that the experience of a parental loss through divorce, death, or other circumstances is a significant risk factor for the development of internalizing disorders, particularly depression.

In considering the hypothesized link between parental loss and depression, three important distinctions in the definition of depression must be considered. First, depression can be defined as a temporary mood state. There is wide agreement that depressed affect and withdrawn behavior are commonly observed as part of children's coping with lengthy separations from, and loss of, an attachment figure (Bowlby, 1980; Rutter, 1981). In this context, however, depression is defined as a transient phase in the process of adaptation, not a fixed outcome. Thus, separation distress is discussed in Chapter 5 rather than here.

A second definition of depression is as a clinical syndrome that occurs during childhood. Despite suggestions that many children from divorced families are clinically depressed (McDermott, 1970), virtually no research has been conducted on this issue. This is not surprising given the controversies surrounding the conceptual and operational definitions of childhood depression. However, interest in this topic has increased recently; research on its relation to divorce and marital conflict may be expected in the near future.

A third definition of depression focuses on functioning during adult life. Depression among adults is a common and reliably defined disorder, and considerable research has been conducted on the possible link between parental loss during childhood and depression during adult life. Empirical support for this hypothesized relation is negligible, however, as discussed below in the section on adult outcomes.

With regard to other internalizing problems experienced during childhood, possible impairments in self-concept have perhaps been studied best, but most investigators have found no differences attributable to family status. In two studies of over 200 children each, no differences in the reported self-concept of middle school (Raschke & Raschke, 1979) or high school (Slater & Haber, 1984) students from divorced and two-parent families were found. However, lower self-concept was related in both these studies to higher parental conflict irrespective of family status. Other researchers have likewise found no differences in self-concept attributable to divorce per se in studies of college women (Hainline & Feig, 1978) and boys aged nine to fifteen (Berg & Kelly, 1979).

In a recent investigation of 11- to 13-year-olds from newly divorced families, some differences in perceived competence were found between children from divorced and married families. In this study, objectively reported self-competence was related to parental conflict but not to family status, while children's perceived competence was related to family status but not to marital conflict (Long, Forehand, Fauber, & Brody, in press). Two other investigations also suggest differences in measures of children's self-concept, but the effects attributable to family status held only when the divorced mothers had not remarried (Parish & Taylor, 1979; Young & Parish, 1977).

While measurement of this elusive construct has been notably difficult, as a group these studies suggest that children's and adolescents' self-esteem is undermined only temporarily, if at all, by divorce. A similarly inconsistent relation exists across various studies of divorce and more clinically relevant internalizing problems among children, such as anxiety disorders and specific phobias (see Emery, 1982). Factors such as the passage of time, parental conflict, and remarriage seem to be more salient predictors.

Despite the pattern of null results, some intriguing, positive findings have been reported. For example, in the original 1976 data and the 1981 follow-up of the National Survey of Children, an increase in self-reported "distress" was found among girls from disrupted marriages (Furstenberg & Allison, 1985). In another analysis of the NSC follow-up data, mothers reported that both boys and girls from divorced families, as well as children from high-conflict, intact families, were more depressed/withdrawn than children from low-conflict, two-parent families (Peterson & Zill, 1986). In considering these findings, it must be noted that the children were seven to eleven years old when first studied and adolescents at the five-year follow-up. It is likely that the self-reports of these age groups are more reliable and valid than those of younger children. Moreover, the large sample size in the NSC study renders effects of small magnitude statistically significant.

While a clear and consistent pattern has not been found for internalizing problems, it would be a mistake to conclude firmly that children of divorce feel no sense of loss and lingering sadness about the marital breakdown, do not worry about themselves, their parents, and day-to-day practicalities, or never cling to fantasies of changing their life circumstances. Many parents and clinicians have suggested that such troubles are quite common. Indeed, self-blame, sadness, fantasies of marital reconciliation, loneliness, and embarrassment are among the most notable concerns reported by sensitive clinical investigators, such as Wallerstein and Kelly (1980). Are such clinical observations inaccurate, or are inadequate measures and research designs responsible for the failure to document important internalizing difficulties?

Wallerstein and Kelly (1980) have made an intriguing observation that may be relevant to the inconsistent findings for internalizing problems. They believe that the parents interviewed were often unaware of the emotional turmoil their children were experiencing as a result of divorce. Because their own feelings were often disparate, the parents were simply not attuned to their children's emotional state. If this finding is true, lack of sensitivity could be one reason why children's internalizing problems have been more difficult to document empirically. Divorced parents are often used as raters of their children's emotional states; but how can they provide accurate judgments about feelings they do not recognize?

Taking a broader view, it may be that the relative absence of documentation of internalizing problems is due to unreliable measurement of these conditions. Whether or not it is a result of parents' lack of awareness, children's internalizing problems are assessed less reliably than are externalizing difficulties (Achenbach, McConaughy, & Howell, 1987). When scales have different reliabilities, what appears to be a substantive difference in their correlations with a third measure may be solely the result of error variance stemming from attenuation due to unreliability in measurement. In the present context this means that differential reliability may be one reason why internalizing is a less consistently documented outcome of divorce than is externalizing.

Several other factors may explain the inconsistent findings for internalizing. One possibility, of course, is that these difficulties are not an important or frequent outcome of a parental divorce, although this conclusion is difficult for many to accept. A related alternative is that internalizing problems frequently accompany divorce, but they abate more rapidly than do conduct disorders. Children's reactions to the acute distress of separation from an attachment figure must be distinguished from their responses to the chronic stressors associated with divorce (Emery, 1982; Rutter, 1971). Depression, anxiety, and unrealistic fantasies may be common but short-lived reactions to the separation process, whereas conduct disorders are associated with more chronic stressors such as unremitting conflict or declines in family income. Along these lines, it is interesting that, compared to children from two-parent families, Felner and his colleagues (1975) found more externalizing problems among children from divorced families, but more internalizing difficulties among children who had lost a parent through death.

Finally, it may be that externalizing problems are more commonly found among boys, and internalizing difficulties more commonly among girls. In concentrating attention on delinquency and aggression among boys, researchers may have tended to overlook the more subtle consequences of divorce for girls.

ACADEMIC COMPETENCE

The intellectual functioning and academic achievement of children from single-parent homes has been of as much concern to researchers and policy makers as has aggression. As with externalizing problems, there is considerable agreement that children reared in single-parent families perform more poorly on a variety of academic measures than do children from two-parent families. Two detailed reviews of a substantial body of studies have concluded that differences are found with sufficient frequency to be considered reliable (Hetherington, Camara, & Featherman, 1981; Shinn, 1978).

The magnitude of the differences found between children reared in these two family forms is typically quite small, however. In their review, Hetherington, Camara, and Featherman (1981) have concluded that the average differences ranged between one and seven IQ points, less than one year of achievement, and about three-quarters of a year of schooling completed. Still, the range of findings obtained has been considerable. Some researchers have found no significant differences, whereas differences as large as 1.6 years in achievement, 0.9 standard deviation units on IQ tests, and 0.8 grade point average units have been reported (Shinn, 1978).

Some have suggested that even the small differences obtained are not due to family structure, but are attributable instead to different socio-economic influences on one- and two-parent families (Herzog & Sudia, 1973). This is an important observation because children from low-income families do perform more poorly on traditional measures of cognitive skills, and they are also more likely to come from single-parent households (Cherlin, 1981; Jencks, 1972).

Although socio-economic status must not be overlooked, it does not fully explain the differences obtained. Several investigators have found that academic differences are less, but still persist, when the effects of social class are taken into account (Featherman & Hauser, 1978; Ferri, 1976; Guidubaldi et al., 1984; Lambert & Hart, 1976; Zill, 1978). For example, in an important study of the number of years of school completed by men born in the United States between 1907 and 1951, consistent differences were found between men reared in one- versus two-parent homes. When surveyed in 1973, men brought up in single-parent families reported having completed a level of formal education that was about three-quarters of a year less than that reported by men who had been reared in two-parent families (Featherman & Hauser, 1978). When socio-economic and racial differences were taken into account, between-group differences in the number of years of schooling were halved, but family status remained a significant predictor.

It is interesting to note that, for men born after 1930, family status became an increasingly more reliable predictor of the number of grades completed than race. For example, for men born between 1932 and 1936, whites completed an average of 0.5 more years of schooling, and men from two-parent families completed 0.75 more years of school. In contrast, for the cohort born between 1942 and 1946, race accounted for only a 0.09 difference in the number of years of schooling, while family status accounted for 0.61 year's difference. In addition, the differences between one- and two-parent families declined for successively later-born cohorts, from about 0.85 years for the oldest group to about 0.60 years for the most recently born men (Featherman & Hauser, 1978). Perhaps this reflects the influence of the increasing state support provided to single-parent families over this time period.

The findings on academic performance discussed so far pertain to single-parent families as a group, not to divorce in particular. Studies of different types of single-parent homes have generally found that divorced children perform more poorly than other single-parent children (Ferri, 1976; Gregory, 1965; Santrock, 1972; Zill, 1978). In turn, children from single-parent nondivorced families do worse than children in two-parent families. Thus, academic difficulties may be partially attributable to characteristics of the single-parent family, but unique aspects of divorce would also seem to account for some of the difference.

A more detailed examination of how children in divorced families differ academically suggests some hypotheses about their cause. Compared to children from two-parent families, children from one-parent households typically obtain significantly lower scores on standardized measures of intellectual capacity and academic achievement, but the absolute magnitude of the difference is quite small. In contrast, when indexed by such measures as teacher ratings, grade point averages, school attendance, and number of years in school, the differences are considerably larger. A recent study of 699 children from 38 states who were evaluated by their school psychologists serves as an example in this regard (Guidubaldi, Perry, & Cleminshaw, 1984). Divorced children were significantly more dependent, disruptive, and unpopular with their peers according to teacher reports; they had a history of lower grades in reading and math and were more likely to have repeated a school grade; and they scored lower on measures of intellectual aptitude and achievement. Differences on the last measures were small in magnitude, however.

Given such findings, it may be that the relation between divorce and academic competence is mediated through behavior in school rather than explained by a direct effect on intellectual capability or performance. Disruptive classroom behavior, altered teacher expectations, or the demands for participation in household routines may make schoolwork and achievement a lower priority for children who must meet the increased practical demands of living in a divorced, single-parent family (Hetherington, Camara, & Featherman, 1981).

SEX-ROLE BEHAVIOR

The changing social climate of the last twenty years has led to a reduced interest in research on the sex-role behavior of children reared in divorced families. Unlike some of their predecessors, contemporary psychologists have a preference for androgyny over sex-role stereotyped behavior, although public attitudes do not appear to be so gender-neutral (Feldman, Biringen, & Nash, 1981). Despite this waning of interest, two gender-role research findings deserve consideration. First, some researchers have found that young boys from father-absent families engage in more activities that are traditionally considered to be feminine than do boys from father-present families. Second, children from divorced families, especially girls, may engage in precocious heterosexual activities compared to children whose fathers have died or whose parents are still married.

Masculine Identity

As noted in the discussion of externalizing problems, divorce research has been influenced by theoretical suggestions that fathers' primary contributions to parenting involve the promotion of socialization. In addition to concerns about aggression, father absence was thought to leave boys without a male with whom they could identify (or whose behavior could be imitated), leading to concerns that boys would not develop normative male sex-role attitudes and behavior. At least one link between the hypothesized "feminization" of boys from single-parent homes and the seemingly contradictory, concurrent concern with aggression has been offered: the feminine-aggressive hypothesis. Increased aggression among father-absent boys has been considered overcompensation for their femininized behavior (Miller, 1958).

A fair amount of divorce research has focused on masculine identity, especially among boys who were five or six years old or younger when their parents separated. Consistent with theoretical predictions, boys, but not girls, from divorced and single-parent homes have been found to have less traditional same-sex preferences as indexed by measures such as game choices and sex-role orientation checklists (Biller, 1969; Biller & Bahm, 1971; Hetherington, Cox, & Cox, 1982; Santrock, 1970). Still, the differences found have generally not been large in magnitude; the findings bear questionable relation to later sex-role behavior and have warranted less concern as social attitudes about the appropriate behavior of men and women have broadened (Herzog & Sudia, 1973). Moreover, the link between sex-role orientation and aggression may have a more parsimonious explanation than the feminine-aggression hypothesis. Both findings may simply reflect the lesser influence fathers exert on child development following divorce (Hoffman, 1971).

Heterosexual Relationships

While concern about the masculine identity of boys from divorced families has waned, the potential link between parental divorce and premature or problematic relationships with the opposite sex has begun to attract more interest. Evidence that children whose parents divorce are more likely to divorce themselves (discussed in the section on adult outcomes) is probably the most influential reason for this. Furthermore, recent psychological theorizing about fathers' contributions to the sexual behavior of both boys *and* girls has contributed to this growing interest (Huston, 1983).

In attempts to explain the intergenerational transmission of divorce, several different developmental hypotheses have been suggested. A debate has emerged over whether children, especially girls, from divorced families: (a) learn ineffective ways of behaving in heterosexual situations that require intimacy or conflict resolution, (b) acquire more liberal attitudes about the acceptability of divorce, (c) are less comfortable in heterosexual situations because of problematic relationships with their fathers, or (d) are at risk for relationship difficulties only because of third variables such as personality characteristics or the restricted availability of desirable partners. While researchers are far from teasing apart these alternative hypotheses, some intriguing research has emerged.

In a study of early adolescents, Hetherington (1972) found that girls whose parents had divorced were precocious and provocative in their interactions with males. Evidence supporting this conclusion came from multimethod assessments, which included unobtrusive observations of a school dance and structured interactions with male experimenters in laboratory situations. In contrast, girls whose fathers had died were shy and reserved with members of the opposite sex, while the interactions of girls who lived with their two biological parents were intermediate between the other two groups. One possible explanation of these findings is that both single-mother groups were more anxious in heterosexual situations, but family circumstances altered the way in which the anxiety was expressed.

In a study of college students, Greenberg and Nay (1982) also found that, compared to children from two-parent families, those from divorced homes were more active and students who had had a parent die were less active heterosexually. In examining possible mediating factors, no differences between groups were found in their recognition or resolution of heterosexual conflict, but the divorced group expressed somewhat more liberal attitudes about the acceptability of divorce.

In another study of college students, men and women from divorced families were significantly more likely to report frequent dating, premarital sex, and cohabition with a member of the opposite sex (Booth, Binkerhoff, & White, 1984). Past parental conflict or troubled parent-child relationships were related to increased sexual activity in the divorced group, while current, not past, problems in these areas were related to dissatisfaction with dating. Students whose fathers had died were comparable to students from two-parent families in dating indices. Students whose parents were unhappily married generally were more active heterosexually, but the differences were not as large or as consistent as for the divorced group.

While these three studies suggest that family composition may have specific effects on heterosexual behavior, a recent, prospective study by Newcomer and Udry (1987) raises the possibility that increased sexual activity is best conceptualized as a form of externalizing, acting out behavior. In a two-year follow-up of 1,405 white, virgin adolescents who were 12–15 years old when first interviewed, boys who changed from two-parent to single-parent families during this time were found to be more likely to have initiated sexual intercourse. For girls, however, it was those who remained in single-parent families who were more sexually active. While neither mothers' or children's attitudes toward sex nor measures of parental control predicted sexual activity, it was paralleled by increases in minor deviance (e.g., cigarette smoking, alcohol use). Since early sexual activity is often part of a pattern of adolescent externalizing behavior, these findings suggest the possibility that an increase in heterosexual activity is best considered as part of the documented increase in externalizing.

Selection factors also may influence or account for the intergenerational transmission of divorce. It has been found that women whose parents have divorced marry at an earlier age, are more likely to be pregnant at the time of marriage, and have more first husbands who were previously divorced (Mueller & Pope, 1977). Not surprisingly, they also have higher divorce rates. The restricted pool of mates, rather than their own approach to heterosexual relationships, may therefore explain the findings. While this suggests yet another alternative interpretation of the observed relation, irrespective of the mechanism of effect, this handful of studies suggests an intriguing area for further research.

SOCIAL COMPETENCE

While considerable effort has been directed toward studying the problems of children whose parents have divorced, surprisingly little research has focused on the adaptive skills of such children. It may be that divorce has its greatest impact on children in that it disrupts the development of such skills, or the converse may be true. One of the more intriguing hypotheses about the effects of divorce on children is Robert Weiss' (1979a) suggestion that it makes them "grow up a little faster." Because of increased practical and emotional demands, as well as changes in the family's authority structure, divorced children may have to assume responsibilities at an earlier age than their peers (Colletta, 1979). This may cause them to become precociously competent in social and practical matters (Weiss, 1979a).

A study of a nonclinic sample of children living in two-parent families is intriguing in this regard (Block, Block, & Morrison, 1981). In this longitudinal study, a measure of parental agreement over child-rearing practices, completed when children were three years old, predicted lower levels of aggression in school among boys at ages three, four, and seven, whereas agreement tended to be associated with *higher* levels of externalizing among girls. Of even more interest, higher levels of *dis*agreement predicted some *increases* in social competence among girls but not among boys (e.g., empathic relatedness, resourcefulness, protectiveness of others) (see Table 4.1). While not designed to test this hypothesis, this pattern of findings can be interpreted as being consistent with the "growing up faster" hypothesis. When conflict arises between parents, perhaps girls respond to the stress with increased prosocial behavior, whereas boys tend to respond with increased aggression and noncompliance.

TABLE 4.1

Correlations of Mother-Father Agreement over Child-rearing Practices
with Teacher Ratings of the School Behavior of Boys and Girls

	Boys			Girls		
	Age 3	*Age 4*	*Age 7*	*Age 3*	*Age 4*	*Age 7*
Scales						
Empathic relatedness	.47**[t]	.24[t]	−.11	−.17[t]	−.36[t]	−.06
Task oriented	.53***[t]	.32*	.41**	.09[t]	−.04	.04
Externalizing vulnerable	−.36*	−.28[t]	−.05	.06	.24[t]	.31
Undercontrol	−.49**[t]	−.43**[t]	−.25[t]	.25[t]	.37**[t]	.25[t]
Compliance	.26	.15[t]	−.02	−.12	−.39**[t]	−.33
Lack of resourcefulness	−.26	−.22[t]	.09	.09	.43**[t]	.32
Interpersonal relatedness	.38*[t]	.08	−.09	−.24[t]	.03	.09
Single Items						
Restless, fidgety	−.53***[t]	−.35*[t]	−.20	.10[t]	.12[t]	−.09
Protective of others	.33*[t]	.05[t]	−.32	−.29*[t]	−.39**[t]	−.08
Behaves sex-typed ways	−.47**[t]	.03	−.58**	.04[t]	−.24	−.24
Immobilized under stress	−.34*[t]	−.27	.00	.16[t]	−.06	.02
Inappropriate emotions	−.36*[t]	−.35*	−.03	.09[t]	−.04	−.03
Open and straightforward	.04	.37*[t]	−.09	.10	−.16[t]	.09

Increasing scores indicate increasing agreement on child-rearing between parents.

[t] Statistically significant difference between correlations for boys and girls. (Only scales or items for which at least one significant sex difference was obtained are reprinted here.)

*p<.05; **p<.01; ***p<.001 that correlation is significantly different from zero.

SOURCE: J.H. Block, J. Block, and A. Morrison, 1981. Parental agreement-disagreement on child-rearing orientations and gender-related personality correlates in children, *Child Development*, 52, 970.

While such an interpretation is intuitively appealing, it must be admitted that it is speculative. Despite some astute clinical observations, the "growing up faster" notion has yet to be convincingly documented. Moreover, if increased maturity and social competence are found among children whose parents have divorced, it is not clear whether this is a desirable or an undesirable outcome. While the words "increased maturity" have a favorable connotation, demands for early competence may deprive children of the opportunity to engage in activities that have less immediate benefit but serve them well in the long run.

ADJUSTMENT DURING ADULT LIFE

In addition to consequences that are apparent during childhood, some of the effects of a parental divorce may be delayed and not become evident until years later. While this possibility raises the interesting question as to what psychological influences might mediate this long-term outcome, the first step is to attempt to document hypothesized associations.

Parental Loss

As noted earlier, it has been suggested that the experience of parental loss during childhood increases the risk of problems in adult mental health, particularly depression. Rationales behind the parental loss hypothesis are often based on psychoanalytic theory and the important conceptual work of John Bowlby on attachment, separation, and loss (1973, 1980). Despite some intriguing speculation based on these perspectives, however, a substantial body of epidemiological research has failed, by and large, to reveal a strong relation between childhood parental loss and adult depression. Two extensive reviews of the literature have concluded that the link has not been unequivocally demonstrated (Crook & Eliot, 1980; Tennant, Bebbington, & Hurry, 1980). Several researchers have found no significant association between childhood loss and adult depression, and because of problems in selecting appropriate comparison groups, identifying and controlling for relevant third variables, and adequately defining the criterion variable, many questions have been raised about research in which such a relation has been reported.

Even if parental loss is causally linked to depression during adult

life, the inconsistency of existing research indicates that its importance must not be great. Moreover, the category "parental loss," like
"father absence," is diffuse and includes a wide variety of family
constellations. In this vein, much as with the divorce literature, family
process is receiving more attention than family structure in parental
loss research. It was recently suggested that the important etiological
link with adult depression is not the experience of parental loss per
se, but the quality of the intervening parental care (Harris, Brown, &
Bifulco, 1986).

Surveys of Adult Adjustment

A different approach in searching for delayed effects has been
taken in a handful of recent, large-scale, survey studies. Here the
focus is on the experience of a parental divorce during childhood and
adult adjustment in a variety of domains. While this research suggests
much smaller effects than some theories predict, some links have
been found.

Kulka and Weingarten (1979) analyzed data from the 1957 and
1976 national probability surveys of adult mental health and found
some small, but statistically significant, differences between adults
who did and did not experience a parental divorce as children.
Mental health utilization was slightly higher among the parental
divorce group, but this was statistically significant only for women in
the 1957 sample (25% vs. 15%). More notable between-group differences were found on other adjustment variables, especially measures
of stress. Adults whose parents had divorced more often reported
feeling high anxiety at times, were more likely to say that bad things
frequently happened to them, and more commonly said they found
bad events difficult to handle. They were also more likely to report
that childhood had been the unhappiest time of their life. Not surprisingly, the effects of family status were attenuated when statistical
controls for socio-economic status were introduced, but several
between-group differences remained, particularly for males. Finally,
it is important to note that in this study no relation was found
between parental marital status and adult depression.

In another study of a national sample, Glenn and Kramer (1985)
also found a relation between parental divorce and adult adjustment.
As indexed by responses to single survey questions, adults who had
experienced a parental divorce reported more unhappiness, poorer

health, and less satisfaction with their family, friends, and community than did adults who had been reared by their two parents. Adults who had experienced a parental death during childhood were also included in this study as a further comparison sample. For men, the experiences of a parental death and of parental divorce were equally predictive of adult dissatisfaction, whereas only parental divorce was related to the adult adjustment of women. While only a small proportion of the variance in the adult adjustment items was accounted for by childhood family status, Glenn and Kramer (1985) concluded that the true association was fairly strong, but was limited by restrictions in the possible maximum values of their measures of statistical association.

Intergenerational Transmission of Divorce

No doubt the most consistent finding about the adult outcome of divorce concerns the intergenerational transmission of marital instability. In several studies of large and representative samples, Pope and Mueller (1979) have documented that divorce is 5.0 to 12% more prevalent among adults whose parents experienced a marital disruption, compared to adults who were reared by their two biological parents (see Table 4.2). These findings are consistent across blacks and whites as well as males and females, and cannot be attributed to socio-economic status alone. Moreover, Pope and Mueller (1979) found that loss of a parent as a result of divorce was a better predictor of adult marital status than was loss of a parent through death. Two less obvious findings are also of particular interest. Parental remarriage was associated with a lower divorce rate for males, but with a higher divorce rate among females. Finally, living with a single mother versus a single father was linked to higher divorce rates for both males and females. Because of measurement problems in the black samples, however, both these latter findings were limited to whites.

Kulka and Weingarten (1979) also found evidence for the intergenerational transmission of divorce. Moreover, they reported that married adults whose parents had divorced were more likely to report having experienced problems in their own marriage. Men, but not women, whose parents had divorced, were more likely to view divorce as the best solution to an unhappy marriage and to suggest that they would remarry following a divorce.

Together with the growing literature on the intergenerational

TABLE 4.2

Percentage of Voluntary Marital Dissolution and Parents' Marital Stability

Race and Sex of Respondent	Parents' Marriage	
	Disrupted	Intact
Black Women		
Cran-NORC	41.5	35.6
Parnes	42.4	33.7
Fertility	39.1	32.2
NORC	49.1	40.1
Black Men		
OCG	28.4	33.2
Crain-NORC	33.2	24.0
NORC	40.6	28.1
White Women		
Parnes	24.5	15.1
Fertility	20.8	14.4
NORC	24.9	17.7
White Men		
OCG	20.2	14.9
NORC	26.4	16.2

SOURCE: Hallowell Pope & Charles W. Muller. The intergenerational transmission of marital instability: Comparisons by race and sex. In *Divorce and Separation*, edited by George Levinger & Oliver C. Moles, Copyright © 1979 by the Society for the Psychological Study of Social Issues. Reprinted by permission of Basic Books, Inc. OCG refers to the Occupational Changes in a Generation survey conducted as part of the March, 1962 Current Population Survey; Crain-NORC refers to a 1966 survey by Robert Crain and the National Opinion Research Center; Parnes refers to a 1967 National Longitudinal Survey of Work Experience of Women; Fertility refers to the 1970 National Fertility Survey; NORC refers to the National Opinion Research Center's General Social Surveys of 1972, 1973, and 1974.

transmission of marital violence (Kalmuss, 1984), these studies suggest that parents' marital interactions influence their children's eventual marital-role behavior. Many researchers speculate that modeling is the likely mechanism of transmission; however, the influences of both divorce and of witnessing family violence (Christopoulos et al., 1987) appear to take different forms at different stages in development. This suggests that a mechanism more subtle than modeling must be operating. Marital distress may be perpetuated through its mediating influence on children's personality (Elder, Caspi, & Downey, 1984), or more subtle cognitive influences may account for the transmission. It may be that the scripts for marital-role behavior are written during childhood, but they remain unread until the marriage begins.

SUMMARY

It was suggested at the beginning of this chapter that cross-sectional research on the effects of divorce on children is of value in planning broad policies, in justifying research on family process, and in specifying the conditions under which a relation between divorce and child adjustment problems must hold. Having completed the review of this literature, it seems appropriate to summarize some conclusions with regard to each of these goals.

In terms of policy considerations, divorce is clearly associated with some undesirable outcomes among children: increased utilization of mental health services, more conduct problems, less success in school, and an increased likelihood of eventually getting divorced. Moreover, divorce may be tied to some less obvious or more transient difficulties among children. While these conclusions are a cause of concern, they should not be a cause for alarm. There is no one-to-one relation between divorce and problems in any of these domains. Even though children from divorced and single-parent families are strongly overrepresented among those with some serious problems, the converse is not true. As must be the case because of differing population base rates, those with serious problems are *not* markedly overrepresented among children from divorced families. Thus, if the policy goal is a broad one, such as "wiping out" delinquency or school failure, it would be inappropriate and inefficient to select divorced families as a major target group for intervention. On the other hand, if the policy goal is to ease the fallout of divorce for children, it is clear that there are problems worth attempting to prevent.

Cross-sectional evidence also provides justification for studying family processes, as these may predict individual differences in outcome more reliably than family status alone. In thinking about family processes, it seems important to consider whether the same developmental processes can cause the diverse outcomes reviewed here, whether different processes are responsible for unique outcomes, or indeed, whether the outcomes are as different as they seem. Related to this last possibility, it is intriguing to speculate that some of the outcomes identified most consistently—increased externalizing behavior, poor school grades and conduct, and early sexual activity— may all be indicators of difficulties in the socialization of some children from divorced families.

In addition to differing ties with various indices of children's short- and long-term adjustment, a few other specifications of the cross-sectional relation between divorce and child behavior problems are worth repeating. First, and perhaps most important, support has *not* been found for hypotheses that predict strong associations between family status and children's adjustment problems, especially the "father absence" and "parental loss" rationales. Second, socio-economic and racial factors appear to explain some, but not all, of the differences found between children from single-parent and two-parent families. Third, children from divorced, single-parent families generally have more adjustment difficulties than children from other types of single-parent families. Fourth, some sex differences in outcome are apparent, particularly with regard to increased externalizing problems among boys, and possibly increased internalizing problems, prosocial behavior, and early heterosexual involvement among girls.

Changes in family process that accompany divorce are discussed in the next chapter. Developmental explanations which link family processes to children's outcomes need to be consistent with the epidemiological findings reviewed here.

5

FAMILY PROCESSES
AND CHILDREN'S
DIVORCE ADJUSTMENT

From the review in Chapter 4, it is clear that the outcome of divorce is hardly uniform. Divorce is associated with various short- and long-term emotional, behavioral, academic, and interpersonal difficulties, but children exhibit diverse responses. The most common is eventual adjustment to the new family situation.

In this chapter the relations between several aspects of the divorce transition and children's diverse outcomes are examined and mechanisms of effect discussed. Specifically, the factors considered here are: (1) temporal influences, including children's age at time of divorce, children's current age, and the passage of time; (2) the consequences of separation from an attachment figure; (3) changes in the relationship between children and their residential parents; (4) changes in the relationship between children and their nonresidential parents; (5) children's involvement in conflict between their parents; (6) remarriage; and (7) family economics.

TEMPORAL INFLUENCES: AGE AT DIVORCE, CURRENT AGE, AND PASSAGE OF TIME

In Chapter 3 some methodological issues were raised with regard to documenting temporal influences on children's adjustment to divorce. In this chapter, substantive findings are discussed regarding the relation between children's functioning and (a) their age at time of separation/divorce, (b) their age at time of research study, and

(c) the passage of time. As discussed in Chapter 3, the historical period is another potentially important temporal influence, but it is not discussed here due to the paucity of empirical evidence on this intriguing point in relation to children's divorce adjustment.

Children's Age at Time of Divorce

The question of whether divorce is more or less stressful for children of different ages is an issue of considerable practical relevance, as parents often wonder if they should stay together at least until their children reach a certain age. The question also is central to various theories of child development. Although rationales differ, most views converge in suggesting that divorce is most harmful when children are younger than five or six, the very age range during which it is most common.

Some theoretical views. Psychodynamic theorists have been most forceful perhaps in predicting age-at-separation effects. One psycho-analytic view focuses on the resolution of the Oedipal conflict and the child's subsequent identification with the same-sex parent (Meissner, 1978). Since the father is usually the noncustodial parent and because identification with the same-sex parent is thought to solidify around the age of six, divorces which involve younger children, especially boys, are expected to be particularly harmful. Other psychodynamic theorizing emphasizes object relations and the importance of having a single "psychological parent" (Goldstein, Freud, & Solnit, 1973). Because the need for stability is thought to be particularly acute for young children, disruptions in the continuity of their relationship with the psychological parent are said to be most disruptive when children are preschoolers.

Some developmental theories also predict that children's age at the time of separation/divorce is important to their subsequent adjustment. Attachment theory and cognitive perspectives are the most prominent of these hypotheses.

Attachment theory has been influential in the understanding of children's adjustment to divorce on at least two levels. As discussed later, attachment theorists have provided a valuable description of the process that children pass through as part of their acute adaptation to separating from an attachment figure. More relevant to the present discussion, attachment theorists have also suggested that the formation of secure attachments early in life is essential for healthy functioning later on. Parent-child bonds in the preschool years, especially during infancy, are held to be particularly important to the development of secure "working models" of other interpersonal relationships (Ainsworth, 1979; Bowlby, 1973). Since attachment to the primary caretaker (usually the mother) is considered most important, and because divorce most commonly involves separation from the father, predictions about the effects of divorce based on the attachment theory are muddied. Nevertheless, to the extent that divorce results in separation from an attachment figure, the theory predicts divorce as being more detrimental for young children.

While not always specifically grounded in a theory of cognitive development, the explanations that children construct about their parents' divorce have also been taken as important predictors of later adjustment. Since children of different ages have different cognitive capacities, age at the time of divorce is thought to mediate adjustment. Wallerstein and Kelly's (1980) observations, in which Piagetian influences are apparent, are perhaps most notable in this regard.

According to Wallerstein and Kelly (1980), three- to five-year-old children are commonly bewildered by divorce. Their limited cognitive capacities prevent them from fully understanding its meaning and implications, leading to unusual fantasies, fears of abandonment, emotional neediness, and aggressive acting out. Of particular note is the suggestion that the egocentricity which characterizes this stage of cognitive development causes children to blame themselves for the divorce and to feel responsible for promoting a reconciliation.

The improved understanding of children who are six to eight years old is thought to promote their greater acceptance of divorce. Grief is said to replace denial. Although it appears that fewer children of this age blame themselves, yearning for the departed parent and fantasies of reconciliation are said to be prominent nevertheless (Wallerstein & Kelly, 1980).

Contrary to their expectations, Wallerstein and Kelly (1980) concluded that children who are nine to twelve years old at the time their parents divorce, adjust quite well compared to six- to eight-year-olds. This finding surprised the authors because cognitive theories do not predict a shift at this age. According to the investigators, however, nine- to twelve-year-olds demonstrate a clear understanding of their parents' divorce and an equally clear disapproval of it. Their anger at their parents for divorcing is conscious, and their social awareness sufficiently developed that embarrassment and attempts at masking emotions are prominent.

Finally, adolescents are said to have the most complete and abstract conception of the reasons for their parents' divorce, which facilitates their adjustment to the event. According to Wallerstein and Kelly (1980), perhaps the most difficult cognitive task for adolescents is to integrate the divorce experience with their developing identity, particularly in relation to heterosexual relationships.

In general, while attachment and cognitive perspectives emphasize process more than psychodynamic models do, all the theories on age-at-separation effects can be criticized for their focus on the event of divorce. Indeed, an event perspective is implicit in the concern about age-at-separation effects. For example, the observations of Wallerstein and Kelly (1980) clearly reflect sensitivity to developmental differences in children's understanding of divorce, and provide valuable insights into how parents might talk to their children of different ages. Still, children's beliefs about the reasons for the divorce surely change over time, as a result of their continuing experiences with their parents and their developing cognitive capacities. While a four-year-old definitely construes divorce differently than a fourteen year old, their changing views of the divorce over time, together with intervening changes in the family environment, are probably more important to their adjustment than their initial cognitive constructions. Psychodynamic views can be similarly criticized since children continue to have contact with their fathers, have relationships with other men, and adapt to different caretakers over time.

Empirical efforts. In addition to these general criticisms, if there are dramatic age-at-separation effects, they have still not been demonstrated empirically. While theorizing about the effects of children's age at the time of divorce certainly raises a number of intriguing questions, research on the topic is equivocal. Based on one or another theoretical rationale, researchers have typically compared children who were younger than five or six years old when their parents separated or divorced, with children whose parents' marriage broke up after that age. Some investigators, as predicted, have found more problems among the early-divorce group (Furstenberg & Allison, 1985; Hetherington, 1972), but others have found no effect (Power, Ash, Schoenberg, & Sorey, 1974), and still others have found more problems among children whose parents divorced *after* this age (Gibson, 1969; McCord, McCord, & Thurber, 1962). Moreover, investigations of specific issues, such as the extent of self-blame at different ages, have found developmental patterns that are far from uniform (Kurdek & Berg, in press).

Because of the confounds between age at separation, current age, and time lapsed since separation, the contradictory pattern of findings should not be surprising. What is surprising, though, is the virtual lack of attempts to untangle the independent effects.

An analysis of the first (1976) and second (1981) waves of the NSC data by Furstenberg and Allison (1985) is a notable exception. As well as providing an interesting set of substantive findings, this report is of considerable heuristic value. Compared to children from two-parent families, children whose parents separated when they were younger than age six were found to have more adjustment problems in both 1976 and 1981 than children who were six or older at separation. Because it is precisely determined by current age and age at the time of separation (see Chapter 3), adjustment also had to be related to the time passed since separation. Indeed, it was, but in a direction opposite to that commonly predicted. More difficulties were found among children whose parents had been separated for a *longer* period of time.

In an attempt to untangle the effects of the confounded temporal variables, Furstenberg and Allison (1985) compared the 1976 and 1981 adjustment of the early and late separation groups. If time since separation was the more important explanatory variable, then both groups should have been more poorly adjusted in 1981 than in 1976. If anything, however, the reverse pattern held. In support of both the early-divorce hypothesis and the prediction that children's adjustment improves over time (see below), differences between both the early- and late-divorce groups and an always-married group tended to diminish, not increase, over time. To their credit, the investigators noted that the greater adjustment difficulties found for the early-divorce group at both times might be attributable to a number of third variables. For example, it is possible that more conflictual marriages end sooner. If so, increased conflict, not early separation, could be responsible for the more adverse outcomes among children.

Children's Current Age

Empirical evidence on age-at-separation effects is scant, but at least theory on this topic is rich. Despite considerable interest in the potential influence of children's current age on their adjustment to divorce, there is little compelling research *or* theory on this topic. The body of research on divorced children of different ages is surprisingly small, and available studies have made no attempt to deal with the temporal confounds. Moreover, there is little in the way of theory that predicts specific age effects when children's age at separation and the passage of time are controlled. It may be that children of divorce experience increased difficulties in comparison to their same-age peers during certain developmental periods (e.g., more anxiety in heterosexual relationships during adolescence), but these types of questions have received little attention.

One finding with regard to current age is worthy of at least a brief note. Some evidence suggests that adolescents from divorced families have less notable adjustment difficulties than younger children (Kurdek, Blisk, & Siesky, 1981). However, because of limited research, this finding cannot be viewed as reliable, and even if it could be, its explanation would not be clear. A host of possibilities are tenable. Adolescents may have fewer problems because it has been longer since their parents divorced, they may rely more on extra-familial support, they may have a more sophisticated understanding of their parents' relationship, or their more elaborate intrapsychic defenses may enable them to mask most of the anxieties they feel.

Passage of Time

While evidence on current age and age at time of separation is equivocal, research on the influence of the passage of time is more conclusive. As time passes, the troubles children have in adjusting to a divorce diminish.

The most careful and influential evidence on this point comes from the longitudinal study conducted by Mavis Hetherington and her colleagues (Hetherington, Cox, & Cox, 1982). In this study, 36 boys and 36 girls from white middle-class families were assessed two months, one year, and two years subsequent to their parents' divorce. An equal number of children of the same age and sex from two-parent families were also followed longitudinally. All children in the study were enrolled in nursery school at the time of the first assessment, and families were evaluated on a number of interview, self-report, and observational measures.

One of the major findings of this investigation concerned the changes in children's adjustment over time. At the two-month assessment, children from divorced families had more difficulties than married children, particularly in the areas of aggression and noncompliance. A deterioration in their functioning was noted at the one-year follow-up, but, although differences due to family status still remained, the children from divorced families showed improvement by the time of the two-year assessment. Data illustrating this changing pattern are presented in Table 5.1. The greater compliance of girls versus boys, and the increased effectiveness of paternal versus maternal discipline are also worth noting in this table.

TABLE 5.1
Children's Compliance to Three Types of Parental Commands

Percentage of Compliance to Parental Commands (Positive)

| | Divorced Families | | | |
| | Girls | | Boys | |
	Father	Mother	Father	Mother
Two months	51.3	40.6	39.9	29.3
One year	43.9	31.8	32.6	21.5
Two years	52.1	44.2	43.7	37.1

| | Married Families | | | |
| | Girls | | Boys | |
	Father	Mother	Father	Mother
Two months	60.2	54.6	51.3	42.6
One year	63.4	56.7	54.9	44.8
Two years	64.5	59.3	57.7	45.3

Percentage of Compliance to Parental Commands (Negative)

| | Divorced Families | | | |
| | Girls | | Boys | |
	Father	Mother	Father	Mother
Two months	47.0	34.8	35.6	23.4
One year	39.1	27.2	28.3	17.2
Two years	49.9	39.7	39.7	31.8

(continued)

Table 5.1 (continued)

Married Families

	Girls		Boys	
	Father	Mother	Father	Mother
Two months	55.7	49.3	47.5	38.4
One year	59.2	51.5	50.3	38.8
Two years	60.5	54.6	53.6	39.0

Percentage of Compliance to Parental Reasoning and Explanation

Divorced Families

	Girls		Boys	
	Father	Mother	Father	Mother
Two months	41.3	29.2	29.6	18.4
One year	26.3	23.1	24.5	14.1
Two years	50.3	42.5	41.4	36.9

Married Families

	Girls		Boys	
	Father	Mother	Father	Mother
Two months	49.1	43.3	41.0	31.1
One year	55.4	48.0	46.2	34.5
Two years	62.3	58.1	58.1	47.6

SOURCE: E.M. Hetherington, M. Cox, and R. Cox (1982). Effects of divorce on parents and children. In *Nontraditional Families*, edited by M.E. Lamb, Hillsdale, NJ: Erlbaum, p. 253. © Lawrence Erlbaum Associates, reprinted by permission.

In a six-year follow-up, Hetherington, Cox, and Cox (1985) found that boys who remained in single-parent, mother-custody families continued to be less compliant than boys in two-parent families. Boys who had conduct problems six years later, however, were not necessarily the same ones who had problems earlier. In fact, behavior problems remained far more stable among children in two-parent families. Divorced families experienced more significant life events during this interval, and these factors were related to changes in their children's adjustment (Hetherington et al., 1985).

Others who have conducted longitudinal studies of divorced families have also concluded that children's and parents' adjustment improves with time (e.g., Ambert, 1984; Furstenberg & Allison, 1985). Wallerstein and Kelly (1980) found that 18 months after the divorce many of the children they were studying had improved. As in the Hetherington study, however, more boys than girls continued to have problems. Five years after the divorce, current life circumstances were associated with the children's adjustment, while events that had occurred at the time of the divorce were not (Wallerstein & Kelly, 1980). Finally, in a 10-year follow-up, Wallerstein (1985) noted that the majority of the children she had interviewed were functioning adequately, even though an excess of delinquency, precocious sexual involvement, and early independence were evident. Perhaps Wallerstein's most significant finding was that feelings of sadness and anger continued to pervade the children's comments about the divorce itself. This was particularly true for children who were older at the time of divorce, the group that was best adjusted when initially studied.

Children's predivorce adjustment. As changes in children's postdivorce functioning with the passage of time have been documented, it has become increasingly important to ask whether at least some of the difficulties *preceded* the divorce. If so, they clearly cannot be a consequence of divorce per se.

Very recently, data from Jeanne and Jack Block's longitudinal study were used to address this vital question (Block, Block, & Gjerde, 1986). Children entered this study of normal social development when they were preschoolers in 1969–71, and were assessed at ages 3, 4, 7, and 14. Because a number of their parents divorced after the study began, a prospective analysis of effects of divorce on children was possible.

In addressing the issue of predivorce adjustment, children whose parents were living together at the time of each assessment but who subsequently divorced, were contrasted with children whose parents remained married throughout the study. Children whose parents had already divorced were eliminated from the analysis and hence it was a truly prospective study. At each assessment, significant differences were found between the always-intact and the to-be-divorced groups. In particular, increased undercontrolled behavior was found among boys as many as 11 years prior to their parents' divorce (Block, Block, & Gjerde, 1986).

Comparable findings were reported in another longitudinal study (Lambert, Essen, & Head, 1977), but no pre- *or* postdivorce differences were found for children whose parents divorced between the 1976 and 1981 NSC interviews (Furstenberg & Allison, 1985). While the important question of children's predivorce functioning therefore cannot be said to be answered, the implications of these initial findings may prove to be far-reaching. They underscore the point that family processes are critical to children's adjustment to divorce, and suggest that at least some disruption begins before the parents physically separate. Having made this crucial point, the specific consequences that might stem from separation from a parent are considered next.

SEPARATION FROM AN ATTACHMENT FIGURE

Some theorists have hypothesized that children's separations from, and losses of, attachment figures cause short-term distress and also lead to an increased risk for problems in later interpersonal relationships (Bowlby, 1973). As reviewed in Chapter 4, however, the empirical literature raises doubts about the role of loss or separation per se in explaining long-term psychological disorder. While this clearly contradicts some earlier predictions (Bowlby, 1951), contemporary views of attachment theorists increasingly emphasize the importance of the quality of children's relationships with multiple caregivers rather than the constant presence of a single caregiver (Ainsworth, 1979; Bowlby, 1979; Harris, Brown, & Bifulco, 1986). Unfortunately, little research has been conducted on effects of separation/divorce on children's attachment to their parents and, in any event, this new focus emphasizes parent-child relationships (discussed below) not separation or loss per se.

In contrast to the literature on long-term outcomes, research on the immediate consequences of separation from an attachment figure is relatively clear and may hold important implications for some of children's reactions to separation/divorce. A three-stage "acute distress syndrome" of upset (protest), followed by apathy or depression (despair), and subsequent loss of interest (detachment), is a well-documented reaction to prolonged separations from attachment figures, especially among preschool children (Bowlby, 1973; Rutter, 1981). There is considerable debate as to whether the detachment stage foreshadows future difficulties (Bowlby, 1973) or indicates adaptation to the new situation (Rutter, 1981). This debate focuses on long-term outcomes, however, and not on the present concern with the process itself.

Based on the attachment literature, children, especially preschoolers, should be expected to experience normal separation distress when the marital separation first occurs. Separation distress may also be expected during visitation exchanges, with very frequent changes, unpredictable schedules, and erratic contact with the nonresidential parent being particularly distressing. Because separations and reconciliations are common (Kitson & Langlie, 1984), children's uncertainty surrounding their relationships with their nonresidential parents can be prolonged, and episodes of separation distress may be repeated. Together with the parents' own ambivalence about the divorce, this can delay children's acceptance of the end of the marriage and fuel their fantasies that their parents will reunite.

While separation distress is a useful construct for understanding emotional disruptions, it has not been systematically studied in the divorce context. Many characteristics of the environment influence the severity of separation distress (Bowlby, 1973), and divorce entails a number of changes in family circumstances in addition to separation experiences.

CHILDREN'S RELATIONSHIPS WITH THEIR RESIDENTIAL PARENTS

While the physical separation of the parents may be the most obvious and acutely distressing aspect of divorce, it does not have the most psychologically salient long-term influence on children. One set of factors that appears to be more important are the changes that can occur in children's continuing relationships with their parents. While many parents work hard to maintain stability in these relationships, strains are frequently reported. This is particularly true during the first few years following the divorce when emotional and practical demands on family members are at a peak. Disruptions in child-rearing are so common and so dramatic that this has been referred to as a time of "diminished parenting" (Wallerstein & Kelly, 1980).

Parenting problems are not uniform across divorced households, across mothers and fathers, or even for one parent across time. Men and women can face very different hurdles, each commonly having greater difficulties in the role traditionally fulfilled by the opposite-sex partner (Luepnitz, 1982). More importantly, the challenges encountered by residential and nonresidential parents differ dramatically. One parent can be overwhelmed with the tasks of single parenting, while the other feels cut off and detached from the children.

Let us now focus on mothers as residential parents and fathers as nonresidential parents. This reflects both the existing psychological literature, as well as the living situation of most divorced children. While the absolute number of father-custody families has risen along with divorce rates, the proportion of father-custody families has remained around 10%. Even when parents share legal custody jointly, children spend most of their time with their mothers (Maccoby & Mnookin, 1986). Hence, father-child relationships and joint custody are discussed further in the section on nonresidential parents. The small body of information on father-custody families and nonresidential mothers is reviewed in the appropriate sections, however.

Mother-Custody Families

In general, the challenges of postdivorce parenting are best conceptualized on the same two levels that characterize children's psychological adjustment: the process of adaptation to change and the outcomes of this process. Both the process of redefinition and the characteristics of the redefined relationship influence children. New homeostatic balances must be achieved in the three content domains of parenting that researchers have identified as the major potential problem areas, namely, affectional relationships, family authority structure, and household task completion. Parents and children may be drawn closer together or distanced in response to the parents' own emotional needs, their perception of the needs of the children, or loyalty dilemmas in the parent-child-parent triad. Not only can specific discipline problems arise, but the basic family authority structure may also be redefined as children assume a degree of independence commensurate with their increased responsibilities. Finally, children may have to "grow up faster" and assume some additional task demands in the single-parent household.

Hetherington's (1986; Hetherington, Cox, & Cox, 1982) longitudinal study of mother-custody families is the most detailed empirical investigation of parenting, and her work generally substantiates the concerns about changes in these content areas. Compared to always-married women, divorced mothers were found to make fewer maturity demands, communicate less well, be less affectionate, more inconsistent, and less effective in controlling their children. Their relationships with their sons were particularly troubled, as boys received less positive feedback and more negative sanctions than daughters.

Parenting problems increased during the first year following divorce, but by the two-year assessment divorced mothers had become more nurturant, consistent, and in better control of their children (Hetherington et al., 1982). As indicated in Table 5.1, changes in parenting practices were reflected in the children's behavior. Children's compliance with instructions first deteriorated then improved over time. Still, children from divorced families remained less compliant than children from two-parent families, even two years after the divorce.

Six years after the divorce, custodial mothers were as affectionate as nondivorced mothers, but they continued to be more negative and less effective in disciplining their sons. Consistent with the "growing up faster" notion, children from divorced families were found to have more power in decision making, greater independence, and were monitored less closely (Hetherington, 1986).

Other investigators have also found that the parenting of custodial mothers is more negative, inconsistent, and less affectionate than that of married mothers (e.g., Burgess, 1978; Colletta, 1979; Wallerstein & Kelly, 1980). In all these studies, however, the variability, as well as the average effects, are important to note. Clinical experience suggests that problems at the opposite extremes are also found. Some residential mothers become overly permissive, rigid, or emotionally dependent upon their children following divorce. Demanding children, guilt, and the absence of a supportive partner can make mothers more susceptible to giving in to children's coercive demands. Loneliness and depression can cause them to seek to fulfill relationship needs through the children, with role reversal, wherein children become the caregivers who nurture their parent, being the extreme example.

Of course, the concern with variability is also a reminder that, after a period of readjustment, most divorced, residential mothers surely function as well as their married counterparts. While the process of redefining the relationship can be stressful for both members of the dyad, there is no one right postdivorce parenting style. A diversity of affectional relationships, discipline practices, and child responsibilities are "healthy" (Maccoby & Martin, 1983). As with two-parent families, long-term difficulties concern problems at the extremes, not in the wide middle range.

Maccoby and Martin's (1983) summary of the work of Baumrind and others is a useful scheme for conceptualizing the long-term influence of different parenting styles on children. They describe four types of parenting derived by dichotomizing and crossing the dimensions of affection and discipline. Authoritarian parents impose many control strategies on their children, but their affectional relationships are weak. This parenting style is associated with less social competence, more withdrawal, and somewhat increased aggression. Permissive parents give much love but demand little discipline. Their children tend to be aggressive, impulsive, and lacking in independence. Uninvolved or disengaged parents are low in both parenting dimensions, and their children seem to have the greatest difficulties, with conduct disorders being a particular problem. In contrast, authoritative parents impose considerable discipline and also give a lot of love, and their children appear to be the best adjusted (Maccoby & Martin, 1983).

For some families, divorce permanently alters parenting from a more to a less adaptive style. Long-term disruptions in parenting and their consequences for children probably depend upon a number of factors, including the mother's emotional well-being, the social and economic support available to her, and the number, ages, and sex of her children. Mothers who are depressed, cut off from kin and friendship support networks, who have more severe economic concerns or a number of young children are more likely to have difficulties (Emery, Hetherington, & DiLalla, 1984). Furthermore, differences within families can be expected. Younger boys are likely to pose greater parenting problems because of their mothers' and their own concerns about their relationship with their fathers, while older girls may become important helpers as they are asked to assume a larger role in parenting younger children and managing household tasks (Weiss, 1979).

Father-Custody Families

While they make up a relatively small percentage of the total, the absolute number of children living in father-custody homes is large. Nevertheless, consideration of father-custody households must begin with a warning about representativeness. Father- and mother-custody families differ on several important dimensions other than custodial status. Compared to noncustodial fathers, fathers with custody have higher incomes and education levels (Chang & Deinard, 1982; Gersick, 1979), are more likely to have a former spouse who is psychologically impaired (Orthner, Brown, & Ferguson, 1976), and are more likely to have older sons living with them (see Chapter 2). Father- and mother-custody families may also differ on numerous unmeasured variables. For example, fathers may be more likely to gain custody after remarrying.

While father-custody families have not been studied in as much detail, the concerns discussed about parenting in mother-custody families are surely applicable to residential parents of either sex. As for differences between mothers and fathers, a general finding is that custodial parents of either sex experience strain in fulfilling tasks traditionally assumed by the opposite sex (Luepnitz, 1982). Confronted with financial burdens, custodial mothers spend more time out of the home and away from the children. Just the opposite occurs for custodial fathers, who have fewer problems with income and more difficulties assuming new parental and household responsibilities. This is not to say that custodial fathers are more involved with their children. In fact, one study found that they used more substitute child care than did custodial mothers (Santrock & Warshak, 1979).

An important point of comparison between father- and mother-custody families concerns the adjustment of the children. Some researchers have been concerned with whether or not children function adequately in their fathers' care. Given the increasing awareness of the importance of fathering, there is no need to address this question here. More relevant is whether children adjust as well, or perhaps better, in the custody of their fathers as of their mothers.

According to Warshak (1986), seven studies have compared the adjustment of children in mother- and father-custody homes, and none have found differences attributable to the custody type per se. The one consistent finding is that children who live with their same-sex parent appear to be better adjusted than those who live with their opposite-sex parent. In one study, father-custody boys and mother-custody girls were found to be more socially competent and more satisfied with their living arrangement than were children who lived with their opposite-sex parent (Santrock & Warshak, 1979). In another investigation, higher rates of delinquency were reported among children living in opposite-sex than same-sex custody arrangements (Gregory, 1965). A similar pattern was reported in two more recent studies not included in Warshak's review. In the NSC, children who lived with their same-sex parent had fewer internalizing and externalizing problems according to parental report, with differences particularly notable for boys (Peterson & Zill, 1986). Similarly, in an intensive, multimethod investigation of a small sample, children who lived with their opposite-sex parent were more aggressive and had lower self-esteem according to several measures of their adjustment (Camara & Resnick, in press, *a*).

In considering the implications of these intriguing findings, it is premature to conclude that subsequent to divorce, boys should be reared by their fathers and girls by their mothers. Because children are not assigned to one or another of their parents at random, selection factors must be carefully considered. For example, fathers who have been particularly involved in parenting may be most likely to get custody of their sons, whereas they may be given custody of their daughters only when the mother has serious psychological problems. While speculative, this alternative explanation of the sex-of-child by sex-of-parent interaction is consistent with social stereotypes.

More to the point, the quality of parent-child relationships is likely to be a better predictor of child adjustment than is custodial status per se. Factors such as low parental conflict, authoritative parenting, and a good relationship with the nonresidential parent have been found to be related to children's healthy functioning in mother- *and* father-custody families (Luepnitz, 1982). This brings us to the next topic: children's relationships with their nonresidential parents and joint custody.

CHILDREN'S RELATIONSHIPS WITH THEIR NONRESIDENTIAL PARENTS

One of the many criticisms of father-absence research is that divorce does not make children "fatherless." Fathers' influence on children's development in both married and divorced families has become a topic of considerable interest to psychologists, and social policy makers have also become very concerned about this relationship. Whether legislative and judicial policies should attempt to influence the extent and quality of children's contact with their nonresidential parent is an issue that is frequently debated in the public forum. As noted in more detail in Chapter 7, joint-custody policies have been designed with the explicit intention of promoting this relationship.

Because research on nonresidential parent-child relationships is intertwined with the joint-custody movement, both literatures are reviewed here. The focus throughout is on nonresidential fathers, since noncustodial mothers have not been studied systematically by anyone.

Frequency of Contact

In considering children's relationships with their nonresidential parents, the first issue to examine is the frequency of contact. The best national data on this issue again come from the NSC. In considering the results of the survey, it is important to bear in mind that: (a) most children in the study were between the ages of 11 and 16 when the follow-up discussed below was conducted, (b) children who were born out-of-wedlock are included in some of the estimates of visitation frequency, and (c) many parents had divorced long before the survey was conducted.

Even with these cautions in mind, the low amount of contact found between children and their nonresidential fathers is startling. According to mother's reports, over 50% of the children in this nationally representative sample had not seen their fathers in the last year, and only 16.4% saw them as often as once a week or more (Furstenberg et al., 1983). As had been found in other studies (Springer & Wallerstein, 1983; Warshak & Santrock, 1983), contact with nonresidential mothers was considerably greater. Thirty-one percent of nonresidential mothers saw their children at least on a weekly basis, and only about 13% had not seen them in the last year (Furstenberg et al., 1983).

A number of factors are related to the degree of contact between children and their nonresidential fathers. Consistent with reports from longitudinal studies (Hetherington et al., 1979), evidence indicates that contact diminished as time passes. When the parents had been separated for less than two years, 45% of the fathers saw their children once a week or more. After 25 to 60 months of separation, 31% of the fathers had not seen their children for a year or more; 41% of the fathers separated 61 to 120 months had not seen their children for over a year; and 64% of the fathers separated for more than ten years had not seen their children for at least a year. The very low frequency of contact for this last group of separated/divorced fathers was as low as that found for never-married fathers (Furstenberg et al., 1983).

More highly educated fathers spent significantly more time with their children, while black fathers spent significantly less time than did whites or other minorities. Not surprisingly, fathers who lived within an hour's drive of their children saw them more frequently. A finding of potential relevance to social policy was that fathers who paid child support visited more frequently than those who paid nothing. Only the fact of paying, not the amount of support paid, was related to visitation frequency. Finally, parental remarriage, particularly remarriage of the mother, was linked to a somewhat lower frequency of father-child contact (Furstenberg et al., 1983).

Quality of Relationships

If nonresidential parent-child visits are infrequent on the average, then what can be said about the quality of the contacts? It has been suggested that this cannot be predicted reliably from predivorce parenting (Hetherington, 1979). Apparently the pain of divorce drives some formerly involved fathers away from the family, while it awakens a dormant interest in others (Hetherington, Cox, & Cox, 1982; Wallerstein & Kelly, 1980).

Available research also supports the common report that much of the interaction between visiting fathers and their children is social in nature, containing less emphasis on discipline, completion of chores, and schoolwork than in two-parent families. On the average, children in divorced families report doing somewhat fewer things with their fathers than do children from two-parent families, but more notable differences are found with regard to discipline. Visiting fathers have more lax rules and lower expectations for their children's conduct (Furstenberg & Nord, 1985). The extreme form of the more indulgent relationship is the "every day is Christmas" pattern, where visits are characterized by frenzied activities designed to fulfill the children's every desire (Hetherington, Cox, & Cox, 1976). Over time, visits do seem to normalize considerably, but divorced fathers continue to be less restrictive than married fathers (Hetherington et al., 1982).

In addition to having fewer demands placed on them, children report feeling less close to nonresidential than residential fathers, but the same is not true of mothers. In the NSC follow-up, 60% of children reported a good relationship with their residential mothers, and 69% a good relationship with their residential fathers. For nonresidential parents, 57% of the children reported a good relationship with mothers, but only 36% did so for fathers (Peterson & Zill, 1986). Importantly, however, even when visits are infrequent and less than ideal, children still regard their fathers as vital figures in their life. Despite the low levels of contact, half of the children in the NSC listed their nonresidential fathers as being members of their family. Only one in twenty of their mothers did so (Furstenberg & Nord, 1985).

While both the quantity and quality of father-child contact can change dramatically, little research has linked this with difficulties or enhancements in children's social, psychological, or academic functioning. The dearth of research is surprising given the diverse and strongly held opinions about the subject. Perhaps even more surprising is that available evidence does not indicate that frequency of contact is clearly related to children's adjustment.

In an analysis of data from the NSC, Furstenberg, Morgan, and Allison (1987) found few significant relations between frequency of contact and a variety of measures of children's adjustment. The null findings held even when measures of closeness with the nonresidential parent and conflict between parents were controlled. Other researchers have also obtained null findings in more intensive investigations of smaller samples (Kurdek, Blisk, & Siesky, 1981; Luepnitz, 1982). Hodges, Wechsler and Ballantine (1979) actually found that frequent visitation was associated with *greater* aggression according to both mothers' and teachers' reports. On the other hand, Hess and Camara (1979) found that visitation duration (but not frequency) was related to improved child adjustment, and Wallerstein and Kelly (1980) and Hetherington, Cox, and Cox (1978) reported that, except when the father was emotionally disturbed or conflict between the parents was very high, more frequent visitation was associated with better adjustment. Further confusion is added by a recent study in which some positive and some negative relations between child adjustment and visitation frequency were reported, with more positive effects recorded when parental conflict was *high* (Kurdek, in press).

Surely factors such as interparental conflict must influence how their relationships with their nonresidential parents affect children. Still, one might expect this relationship to be so important that its value would be evident despite complicating factors. Apparently, this is not the case.

Some research does suggest that it is important for children to have a good relationship with at least *one* of their parents. Higher levels of stress, aggression, and problems in social relationships have been linked to difficulties in children's relationship with one or both parents (Hess & Camara, 1979). Other findings indicate that a good relationship with one parent can buffer the child from the ill effects of a bad relationship with the other (Hetherington, Cox, & Cox, 1979; Peterson & Zill, 1986; Rutter, 1971), but there may be differences between custody arrangements here. In father-custody families, a good relationship with the mother may protect children from a poor relationship with the custodial parent, but in mother-custody families a good relationship with the father is only a partial buffer (Camara and Resnick, in press, *b*). While based on a small sample, this conclusion is consistent with the finding that nonresidential mothers remain more involved with their children than do nonresidential fathers.

In general, it seems premature to conclude that relationships with their nonresidential parents are of little importance to children from divorced families, given the small amount of research that has been conducted. Even if the negative findings were based on several reliable studies, such a conclusion might still be wrong. The majority of the nonresidential fathers in the studies reviewed above were not particularly involved with their children; it is possible that very involved fathers would have a much more important impact. Moreover, in both married and divorced families, much of the influence that fathers have on their children may be indirect and mediated through the mother. Nonresidential fathers may continue to be important to their children through providing or failing to provide support for the mothers' child-rearing efforts, serving or being unavailable to serve as a buffer in mother-child conflicts, or exacerbating/smoothening conflict over child-rearing (Emery, 1982; Emery et al., 1984; Hetherington et al., 1982). Moreover, the tremendous symbolic importance that biological parents hold in the eyes of children cannot be ignored, even if it is difficult to quantify. Despite these considerations, it must be recognized that there is no strong evidence at present for linking children's adjustment with their relationships with nonresidential parents.

Joint-Custody Families

It is ironic to begin a discussion of joint custody after raising doubts about the influence nonresidential parents have on their children, because the importance of this relationship is assumed by joint-custody proponents. On the other hand, this juxtaposition is not surprising since advocacy has preceded rather than followed research on the topic (Clingempeel & Reppucci, 1982). This is true for both the informal practices of innovative parents and the enactment of legislation which increasingly has supported joint custody as an option, sometimes as a preference.

Before considering its implications, it is essential to define joint custody carefully. Two distinctions must be made. In joint *legal* custody, parental rights and responsibilities are shared, but the children typically spend considerably more time with one parent. In joint *physical* custody, not only is legal guardianship shared, but children spend approximately equal time with each parent. By far the most common form of joint custody is joint legal custody (Maccoby & Mnookin, 1986; Phear et al., 1984), and unless noted otherwise, this is the intended meaning of the term as used here.

Some research has been conducted comparing children living under joint- and sole-custody arrangements. This research cannot be conclusive, however, because parents with joint custody are an unusual group—they are older, more wealthy, and better educated than sole-custody parents (Luepnitz, 1982). Parents who choose joint custody may also have a particularly cooperative relationship. Hence, policy makers need to be careful in using research on negotiated joint custody to draw inferences about court-imposed joint custody. Two studies have shown that parents who agreed to joint custody between themselves were more satisfied than parents who settled on joint custody only after court involvement (Irving, Benjamin, & Trocme, 1984; Steinman, Zemmelman, & Knoblauch, 1985).

While these cautions about causal inference raise questions about imposing joint custody on unwilling parents, research on the question is relevant to the discussion of children's relationships with their nonresidential parents. The intention of joint custody is to improve these relationships, an assumption which needs to be tested in its own right. Is joint custody really a new way of co-parenting after divorce, or is it merely a relabeling of traditional postdivorce child-care practices?

Some important differences in the co-parenting of joint- and sole-custody parents have been found, but in general they are not dramatic. Child-care arrangements are more specifically detailed in joint-custody agreements (Phear et al., 1984), contact between nonresidential parents and their children is somewhat greater (Bowman &

Ahrons, 1985; Greif, 1979; Wolchik et al., in press), and fathers are more involved in child care (Bowman & Ahrons, 1985). In most cases, however, the actual child-care arrangements resemble those found in mother custody families, as is suggested by the increase in joint legal custody relative to joint physical custody (Maccoby & Mnookin, 1986).

In addition to promoting children's relationships with each parent, there is hope that joint custody will also facilitate cooperation in postdivorce parenting. This is an especially important goal since greater cooperation is needed when both parents remain involved in child-rearing. Some research does indicate greater cooperation among joint-custody parents, but the evidence is not uniform.

For a number of good reasons, postdivorce litigation rates have often been used as an index of cooperation. In one study, much higher compliance with support awards and fewer court appearances over both visitation and financial disputes were found among parents with joint rather than sole custody; these parents also indicated greater cooperation in their self-reports (Luepnitz, 1982). Better compliance with child-support payments was also found among joint- than sole-custody families in another investigation (Pearson & Theonnes, 1985). Other researchers indicate a lower rate of relitigation of custody or visitation disputes among joint- than sole-custody families (Ilfeld, Ilfeld, & Alexander, 1982), but higher relitigation rates have also been reported (Phear et al., 1984). The fact that all except a small subgroup of parents in one of these studies (Ilfeld et al., 1982) elected for joint custody makes the conclusions that can be reached from this research all the more tentative. Moreover, since joint-custody arrangements are often viewed as an evolving and flexible parenting plan, and sole custody as an attempt at a final solution, perhaps great differences in litigation concerning the children should not be expected.

An even more important issue concerns the adjustment of children in joint-custody families. Numerous descriptive reports have suggested that children can function well even under complex joint-custody arrangements, but systematic research on the topic is sparse (Clingempeel & Reppucci, 1982). In a study of 91 children with either maternal, paternal, or joint custody, no differences were found between groups on measures of children's behavior problems, self-esteem, or psychosomatic problems. Measures of family process, such as the degree of parental conflict, were correlated with children's adjustment within each of the three custody groups, however (Luepnitz, 1982). In another investigation comparing 33 joint-custody and 100 mother-custody families, joint-custody children reported more positive divorce experiences and scored higher on a measure of self-esteem, but no differences were found on parents' ratings of the children's adjustment (Wolchik, Braver, and Sandler, in press). Finally, Shiller (1986) found that 20 boys from joint-custody families were rated by their mothers as having fewer emotional and behavioral problems than 20 boys from mother-custody families. Importantly, teachers also tended to rate joint-custody boys as better adjusted. It is important to note that in this last study, unlike in most research, joint-custody was defined in terms of physical child care—a fairly equal split of the child's time in each household.

Some recent studies have begun to address the important question of predicting which families are and which are not successful in joint-custody arrangements. One study indicates that, in spite of considerable conflict, joint-custody can be successful if mutual parenting respect is maintained, personal feelings are distinguished from the needs of the children, and parental and spousal roles are separated (Steinman et al., 1985).

While providing some support for the option, in general, research does not indicate dramatic effects due to joint custody. Nonresidential parent-child contact may be more frequent, parental cooperation may be higher, and children may function somewhat better in joint- than in sole-custody families. Differences between the custody arrangements are not large, however, and may be attributable to selection factors rather than to joint-custody per se.

Such a conclusion is not intended as a dismissal of joint-custody as a real, perhaps important, change in divorce law. Differences in the adjustment of children in married and divorced families are not large, and there is considerable within-group variability. Thus, comparisons between children living in different custody arrangements cannot be expected to indicate dramatic differences. Moreover, small improvements are better than no improvements at all, and joint-custody may have an important symbolic value to parents and to children which is not easily quantified (Emery, Shaw, & Jackson, in press). Still, like the evidence on nonresidential father-child relationships, it must be acknowledged that existing research does not indicate that joint-custody exerts a strong influence.

INTERPARENTAL CONFLICT

The above discussions focused on children's dyadic relationships with their residential and nonresidential parents, respectively. The parent-child-parent triad is also of considerable interest in understanding children's divorce adjustment. Loyalty dilemmas and inconsistent discipline between parents are common clinical issues for divorced families (Emery et al., in press), and the focus on triads necessitates conceptualizing in systems terms (Minuchin, 1985).

Research on interparental conflict provides an empirical window on family triads, since this literature addresses how the *relationship* between the two parents affects children. This literature is also important because the influence of interparental conflict spans the dissolution process. Divorce is typically preceded by lengthy periods of marital distress; hostilities often escalate at the time of separation and as a result of legal proceedings; and acrimony can continue long after the formal divorce.

In an earlier review, I argued that converging evidence suggests that interparental conflict is more strongly linked to adjustment difficulties among children than is marital status per se (Emery, 1982). This conclusion was based on the evidence that, first, compared to children from homes disrupted by death, children from divorced homes have more psychological problems (Douglas, Ross, Hammond, & Mulligan, 1966; Gibson, 1969; Gregory, 1965); second, children from divorced but conflict-free homes have fewer behavior problems than children whose parents remain in an unhappy marriage (Gibson, 1969; McCord, McCord, & Thurber, 1962; Nye, 1957; Power, Ash, Schoenberg, & Sorey, 1974); third, children from high-conflict divorces have more adjustment difficulties than children from low-conflict divorces (Anthony, 1974; Hetherington, Cox, & Cox, 1976; Kelly & Wallerstein, 1976; Jacobson, 1978; Westman et al., 1970); fourth, problems found among children from broken homes may begin before the parents separate (Lambert, Essen, & Head, 1977); and, finally, similar outcomes (increased undercontrolled behavior), sex differences (more problems among boys), and mediating conditions (the protective effect of a good relationship with one parent) are found among children from high-conflict married and divorced families (Emery, 1982).

A number of additional recent findings support the interparental conflict hypothesis. In a prospective analysis of 1,265 children living in New Zealand, children whose parents had separated and then reconciled had more conduct problems than those who remained in a stable one-parent family (Fergusson, Dimond, & Horwood, 1986). Among the subsample of families who divorced between the two NSC surveys, children from marriages where conflict was high in 1976 exhibited three times more psychological distress in 1981 than children whose parents reported low or moderate conflict before the divorce (Peterson & Zill, 1986). Only children from high-conflict divorced families were psychologically distressed in young adult life according to data from the New York Longitudinal Study (Chess, Thomas, Korn, Mittelman, & Cohen, 1983). No mean differences were found in a comparison of children living in maternal, paternal, and joint-custody families, but interparental conflict was associated with lower self-esteem and more behavior problems in all three groups (Luepnitz, 1982). As noted above, recent evidence indicates that the conduct problems found among boys after divorce may begin several years before the parents separate (Block et al., 1986). Finally, interparental conflict has been found to be a predictor of child adjustment irrespective of family status in numerous cross-sectional studies of smaller, select samples (Christopoulos, Cohn, Shaw, Joyce, Kraft, & Emery, in press; Emery & O'Leary, 1984; Enos & Handal, 1986; Rutter & Quinton, 1984; Shaw & Emery, 1987; Slater & Haber, 1984).

Taken together, the evidence is sufficiently strong to permit a consideration of how, not whether, interparental conflict is tied to the development of negative outcomes among children from divorced families.

Mechanisms of Effect

Theoretically, parental conflict can affect children in a number of direct and indirect ways. Perhaps the most straightfoward is that exposure to conflict is a stressor in its own right. Children as young as eighteen months become upset during angry exchanges between their parents, and by the age of five or six their distress is evident in attempts to intervene in the quarrel (Cummings, Zahn-Waxler, & Radke-Yarrow, 1981; 1984). Even conflict between strangers is distressing, as two-year-olds respond to simulated arguments with notable upset (Cummings, Iannotti, & Zahn-Waxler, 1985). A finding of interest in the experimental data is that boys tend to respond with increased aggression, while girls respond with increased distress, a notable parallel to sex differences in externalizing and internalizing following divorce.

If exposure to conflict is distressing to children, then they are motivated to terminate it, and their successful efforts will be negatively reinforced. Intervening in dyadic conflict poses special problems when the third member of the triad has relationships with the other two, however. There are various pulls in families to ally with one side or the other, as well as good reasons not to form an alliance (Vuchinich, Emery, & Cassidy, in press).

The manner in which children intervene in, or withdraw from, their parents' conflicts, may be important for understanding of the individual differences found among children from divorced families. Family-systems theorists have discussed several problematic possibilities. Minuchin and colleagues (1975), for example, describe three alternatives: children can side with one parent against the other (parent-child coalition), attempt to maintain an equal and balanced relationship with each parent (triangulation), or reunite their parents by serving as a scapegoat (detouring).

Other alternatives seem possible as well. Children may attempt to directly intervene in the conflict and mediate a solution. Emotional or physical withdrawal is another way of relieving the distress that conflict creates (Emery et al., 1984). Other children, aware of the consequences of conflict, manuever to avoid becoming trapped in it (Johnston, Campbell, & Mayes, 1985). Finally, at least a few children surely exploit the division between their parents, playing one off against the other.

Children of various ages may use different ways of intervening in their parents' conflict and may form different alliances. In one study, children of divorced families aged six to eight were more confused in their loyalties, while nine- to twelve-year-olds tended to ally with one parent or the other (Johnston et al., 1985). Also, younger children are probably less direct in their responses to conflict, whereas older children may actively try to mediate a resolution or withdraw from the family altogether. The child's sex may also be influential. Same-sex alliances may be formed, and children surely attempt to influence their parents in ways consistent with gender-role expectations. For example, extreme antisocial behavior may be an effective detouring manuever for boys, whereas for girls, extreme prosocial behavior may better serve the function of uniting the parents in a common focus on the child.

An intriguing study by Cooper, Holman, and Braithwaite (1983) is one of the few empirical investigations of family-conflict patterns. These investigators identified five family types: cohesive two-parent families, cohesive one-parent families, families with a parental coalition (against all the children); divided families (with one parent and at least one child on either side); and the isolated child (alone against all family members). Based on diagrams of these patterns that were presented to them, children identified their family type. According to both child and teacher reports, children's self-esteem was lowest in the divided families, where loyalties were clearly torn, and in the isolated-child families, where the child was the family scapegoat.

Even when children are not directly involved in the conflict, the emotional distancing that occurs between divorcing parents presents children with an inherent loyalty dilemma. How can a close relationship be maintained with two parents who do not like each other? Parents may feed into this dilemma by actively competing for the children, but even when they struggle to keep children out of the middle, conflicting loyalties are likely to be felt. In the NSC, 55% of adolescents from two-parent families reported a good relationship with *both* their parents, versus only 25% of those living with their divorced mothers and 36% of those living with their divorced fathers.

In addition to causing distress and creating loyalty dilemmas, interparental conflict can disrupt children's socialization experiences. Aggression may be learned from witnessing angry parental battles (Porter & O'Leary, 1980), and inconsistent discipline, a factor often linked to the development of conduct problems, is another potential problem area. Discipline can be inconsistent due to parents' lack of agreement about child-rearing philosophies or lack of communication about each other's opinions and actions. Discipline may also be intentionally subversive if child-rearing becomes an arena in which marital battles are fought (Emery et al., in press; Wallerstein & Kelly, 1980). In one exemplary study, parental disagreement about child-rearing predicted children's adjustment difficulties in school several years later. It also predicted subsequent divorce (Block et al., 1981).

The above analysis presupposes conflict that is open, angry, and not hidden from the child, a pattern that is most strongly related to the development of conduct problems (Emery, 1982). Divorced parents must, of course, be expected to be angry with each other, and the expression of that anger may be helpful to their own emotional health. The task for parents is to disentangle their angry feelings engendered by the ending of their roles as spouses from the business of continuing their cooperative roles as parents (Emery et al., in press). Cooperation over child-rearing predicts positive. child adjustment regardless of whether or not the parents are in conflict over other matters (Camara & Resnick, in press, *a*).

REMARRIAGE

Despite the problems that caused their marriage to end, most divorced adults remarry. Surprisingly, however, few researchers have systematically studied the effects of remarriage on children, and what evidence is available is limited almost exclusively to stepfathers. Consequently, our understanding of children's adjustment to this transition is limited. Indeed, Cherlin (1981) has suggested that the fact that so little is known about remarriage is an important source of distress in its own right. The uncertain expectations and the lack of guidance about the role of stepparents makes remarriage an "incomplete institution."

There certainly are doubts about the appropriate role stepparents should play. In general, children feel less close to stepparents than to biological parents (Furstenberg, 1987), and problems have been reported both when stepfathers become involved in parenting too quickly, and when they remain aloof and disengaged (Hetherington et al., 1982). Fathers in longer remarriages are more involved with the children, especially their stepsons, reflecting that relationships can develop over time (Hetherington, 1986). Good relationships seem to be achieved more readily with young children (Wallerstein & Kelly, 1980); teenagers have more difficulty (Hetherington et al., 1982); and teenagers from remarried families may be no better adjusted than adolescents from divorced homes (Steinberg, 1987).

The quality of children's relationships with their custodial parent may mediate the impact of the stepparent. Remarriage may be more beneficial to children when the custodial parent has been depressed (Wallerstein & Kelly, 1980) and, in general, a stepparent may have a more positive influence when single-parenting is troubled. In contrast, children who have a close and involved relationship with their custodial parents have a more difficult time accepting stepparents (Furstenberg & Spanier, 1984).

While the existing empirical literature is fraught with methodological difficulties (Ganong & Coleman, 1984), there is at least some evidence that boys from divorced families experience benefits from remarriage (Chapman, 1977; Oshman & Manosevitz, 1976), while girls react adversely (Clingempeel, Brand, & Ievoli, 1984; Santrock, Warshak, Lindbergh, & Meadows, 1982). The mediating influence of the relationship with the custodial parent may explain the apparent sex difference. Since girls typically draw closer to their mothers following divorce (Peterson & Zill, 1986), it may be that they are more likely to view stepfathers as "intruders," whereas stepfathers may serve as a buffer in the strained relationships between divorced mothers and their sons (Hetherington, 1986).

To summarize, it appears that a stepfather is initially seen as an outsider who threatens mother-child relationships and who has little legitimate authority. Over time, the threat may diminish and more authority assumed, but the balance achieved probably differs from that of always-married families. The parenting influence of stepfathers is typically more indirect and channeled through their support of their wives. In this regard, it should be noted here that stepfathers offer financial as well as emotional support. While divorced mothers often struggle financially, the economic position of always-married and remarried families is similar (Jacobs & Furstenberg, 1986).

In addition to introducing a stepparent to the family, remarriage may have other consequences. Visitation with the nonresidential parent decreases following remarriage, especially when the custodial parent remarries (Furstenberg et al., 1983). Old marital tensions may be rekindled, creating new loyalty dilemmas for children (Wallerstein & Kelly, 1980), or custody battles may be renewed as the remarried parent may feel better able now to care for the children (Furstenberg & Spanier, 1984). Finally, remarriage may be followed by a second divorce. As noted in Chapter 2, the presence of children from a previous marriage is associated with an increased risk of divorce. Furstenberg et al. (1983) found that 37% of the children who entered a stepfamily later experienced the breakup of that family, and 10% experienced three or more marital changes.

ECONOMIC FACTORS

Only the consequences that changing family relationships have for children of divorce have been examined thus far. As mentioned in Chapter 2, divorce also entails a variety of practical changes. The most notable is a lowered standard of living, particularly for divorced women and their custodial children. While most divorced mothers attempt to make up for their loss of income by working longer hours (Espenshade, 1979), their economic problems are of sufficient magnitude to be a growing concern to public-welfare agencies.

In 1948, 25 of every 1,000 children received supplemental income from the Aid to Families with Dependent Children (AFDC) program; death of the father was the most common basis for eligibility. By 1973, this number had increased to 113 per 1,000; today, almost 90% of AFDC recipients have a living parent who is absent from home. In general, families headed by single mothers are more than three times as likely to be impoverished as those headed by a married couple [National Institute for Child Support Enforcement (NICSE), 1986]. The marked increase in out-of-wedlock births clearly contributes to these statistics, but divorce is a major factor. In 1979, 45% of all families qualifying for AFDC were separated or divorced (SCCYF, 1983).

The fact that marital dissolution rates are higher among low-income families explains part of these statistics (Espenshade, 1979). Nevertheless, longitudinal evidence indicates that separation and divorce play a causal role as well. Using data from the Michigan Panel Study of Income Dynamics (MPSID), Hoffman (1977) documented the changing incomes of over 2,400 women. Between 1968 and 1974, the real incomes of couples who remained married increased by 21.7%, while decreases of 29.3% and 19.2% were recorded for divorced women and men respectively. Taking family needs into account, divorced women experienced a 6.7% decline in living standards, divorced men a 16.5% gain, and married couples a 20.8% gain. The fact that women were far more likely to be responsible for the care of children was the single factor most responsible for this difference (Hoffman, 1977).

More recent analyses of the MPSID indicate that the time since divorce and, especially for women, remarriage significantly influence postdivorce economics. Compared with their predivorce living standards, one year following divorce women have only 91% of income relative to their needs, while men have 113%. Five years after divorce women have 110% and men 130% of their income relative to their needs compared to predivorce levels (always-married families have 130%). Divorced women who are still single five years later have only 94%, while those who remarry have 125% (Duncan & Hoffman,

1985). Weitzman's (1981) study of a California sample indicates a much larger discrepancy between the sexes one year following divorce—a 42% increase in income relative to needs for men and a 73% decline for women, but preference is given to the MPSID study here because of its superior sampling, repeated measurement, and longer time lags.

Other analyses of the MPSID indicate that income changes directly affect the percentage of families living in poverty. Of the men and women who remained married between 1967 and 1973, 6.0% moved into poverty during this period, as did 13% of the men who were divorced. Among the women who had divorced and not remarried, however, fully 33% moved into poverty (Duncan & Morgan, 1976a). The sex difference was replicated in a recent analysis of the MPSID. Between 1966 and 1981, 9.9% of white women with minor children had family incomes below the poverty level when married, but that figure increased to 28.7% following divorce. Among nonwhite women, 33.4% were below the poverty line when married, 44.3% after divorce. In contrast, the percentage of men living at poverty levels actually *decreased* following divorce. Among whites, 9.2% men had incomes below the poverty level when married, while 4.8% were impoverished following divorce. Among nonwhite men, 35.7% lived in poverty when married, 26.1% following divorce (Nichols-Casebolt, 1986).

Because they usually are reared by their mothers, most children experience a decline in their standard of living. In the MPSID, children whose parents separated or divorced experienced a 13.8% decline in real family income, compared with a 34.4% increase for children whose parents remained married. Not surprisingly, children who lived with their fathers fared much better than children who lived with their mothers (Duncan & Morgan, 1976b).

A variety of factors contribute to the lower standard of living of divorced families. The greater expense of maintaining two separate households is an obvious one. Because of economies of scale alone, a family of four with an average income would experience an 11% reduction in their standard of living if the parents divorced, the mother had custody, and the father moved into a separate household (Espenshade, 1979). For families living at the poverty level, the economic disadvantage is even greater (Espenshade, 1979).

While two households are more expensive to maintain than one, accounting for the economic discrepancy between divorced men and women is more complex. Part of it is due to the failure to include the value of fixed assets in making financial comparisons. When assets such as the family home are taken into account, the differences between the sexes are not as great (Espenshade, 1979). Nevertheless, disparities remain. Differences in employment rates and in the salaries of employed men and women obviously contribute to the discrepancy, as do these facts: (1) in 90% of divorces children are subsequently in the physical custody of their mothers; (2) the average combined child support and alimony awards are inadequate to maintain mother-headed families at their predivorce income level (Weitzman, 1985); and (3) compliance with support orders is the exception rather than the rule. In 1981, of all single mothers who had been ordered to receive child support, only 47% received the full amount; 28% received nothing at all (NICSE, 1986).

The economic consequences of divorce can set into motion a series of changes that would seem to tax children's coping resources. Important life events may include moving from the family home, changing schools, losing contact with old friends, spending more time in child-care settings while their mother is at work, and dealing with their parents' preoccupation with, and conflict over, financial matters. In fact, it has been suggested that economics alone may account for the psychological difficulties experienced by children following divorce. In their influential review, Herzog and Sudia (1973) noted that socioeconomic controls attenuate or eliminate many of the differences in delinquency, academics, and sex-role behavior found in studies comparing children from father-absent families and father-present households.

While economic factors surely are related to children's adjustment, as reviewed in Chapter 4, differences between one- and two-parent families generally decrease, but do not disappear, when income controls are introduced. Moreover, because lower income is both a cause and a consequence of divorce, it is not clear how it should be controlled statistically. Income *decline*, rather than absolute income level, may be a better predictor of divorce adjustment both for children (Desimone-Luis, O'Mahoney, & Hunt, 1979) and for divorced women (Braver, Gonzalez, Sandler, & Wolchik, 1985).

While it is often taken into account statistically, it is surprising how rarely the relation between income and children's divorce adjustment has been studied directly. Little speculation, let alone empirical evidence, has been offered as to how economic factors might cause increased psychological difficulties. Perhaps the most straightforward hypothesis is that divorced parents with economic problems may experience more task overload than others. In this respect, divorced working mothers, but not married working mothers, have been found to provide less cognitive and social stimulation to their children than married nonworking mothers (MacKinnon, Brody, & Stoneman, 1982). Differences in child-rearing practices were the focus of another study of moderate- and low-income divorced white mothers. Few differences were found between moderate-income divorced and married mothers, except when they had more than one child. In this circumstance divorced mothers made more self-care demands. Numerous differences were found between moderate- and low-income divorced mothers, however, as low-income single mothers made more demands for self-care and obedience. The presence of more than one child and of a male child interacted with income status. Low-income single mothers with multiple children expected the most obedience from their sons, while moderate-income single mothers were most protective of their daughters (Colletta, 1979).

These studies are best viewed as illustrative rather than conclusive, but they are examples of one type of research that needs to be conducted. Other broad questions that need to be addressed are: What factors (e.g., parental conflict, lower father-child contact) are correlated with postdivorce financial difficulties? What are the independent influences of psychological and economic stressors on children's adjustment? Is the absolute level of income or the change from previous financial status most important? What are the mechanisms through which low income or income decline impact on children?

SUMMARY

Substantive evidence on the family changes introduced by divorce have been examined in this chapter. That divorce is a process, not an event, is unequivocally made by these data.

What family processes predict children's adjustment? A handful of factors stand out: the passage of time, the quality of children's relationships with their residential parents, parental conflict, and the economic standing of children's residential family. Equally important are factors for which predictive evidence is not strong: the long-term effects of the separation itself, the child's age, the amount of contact with the residential parent, and, for girls, remarriage.

The family processes discussed here are often difficult to define; they have an influence that is dependent upon a number of conditions; and their interactive effects are not well understood. These observations, together with emerging psychological issues, such as the distinction between marital and parental roles, presage the clinical discussion of individual families in Chapter 6. An examination of the multiple family changes caused by divorce begins to convey a sense of the reorganization of family relationships that occurs after divorce. Recognition of this process is important clinically, and it forces one to consider new psychological perspectives on family systems. Empirically, a basic question this process poses is how the various stressors account for or potentiate each other's effects in influencing children's adjustment. While divorce research provides a useful window on this issue, it is a question of broad importance to the understanding of normal and abnormal child development.

Despite the caveat about individual differences, the evidence reviewed here suggests a list of goals for policy makers to attempt to achieve for the "average" divorced family. Policies should be encouraged if they: (1) help to define a clear and relatively quick ending to the separation phase of divorce, (2) support the relationship between children and their residential parents, (3) secondarily, encourage contact between children and their nonresidential parents, (4) facilitate cooperation and reduce conflict in co-parenting, and (5) offer economic stability to the postdivorce family. Policies which attempt to achieve one of these goals (e.g., stringent enforcement of financial settlements) may tend to conflict with another goal (e.g., parental cooperation). Thus, as discussed in Chapter 7, one must be sensitive to the means, as well as the intended ends, of policy. And, of course, since there is no guarantee that a policy will actually achieve its intended goals, evaluation is necessary.

6

INTERVENING IN DIVORCE: THERAPEUTIC APPROACHES

In this chapter some clinical perspectives on the process of change in the divorced-family system are presented and research on therapeutic intervention in divorce is reviewed. Idiographic clinical observations can enrich appreciation of complexity and diversity, since subtleties that cannot be measured objectively may be noted, changes over time appreciated, and individual differences highlighted. Clinical observations have the potential to be idiosyncratic as well as idiographic, however. In addition to their obvious methodological limitations, they are necessarily biased toward problems rather than strengths. Thus, the present discussion should be tempered with the reminder that the most common outcome of divorce is adjustment to the new family situation.

Research on therapeutic interventions in divorce is a related clinical consideration. Although it is only the average effects that are reported, much of the challenge of outcome research is developing a clinical intervention that is worthy of painstaking study. Even when treatment protocols are standardized, the clinical part of outcome research is inherently idiographic. Unfortunately, most programs designed specifically for divorced families have not been evaluated, and the question of how divorced family members fare in established problem- and theory-focused treatments is rarely asked.

SOME CLINICAL PERSPECTIVES ON THE DIVORCED FAMILY SYSTEM

While research on family process has moved toward an increasingly fine-grained analysis of relationships in the divorced family, clinical observations can add detail to the transitions outlined by empirical research. This clinical discussion also suggests avenues for intervention. Transitions are inherently stressful and institutionalized guidance as to how they should be negotiated in divorce is often not adequate. Support and education, therefore, can be useful intervention techniques. Issues specific to the individual family may be resolved, and the divorce process can be "normalized" by reassurances that certain challenges are a common part of the transition.

In considering the clinical literature on divorced families, a major distinction to make is whether the issues are conceptualized at the individual, dyadic, or triadic level of analysis. While these different foci are not necessarily incompatible, they often reflect psychodynamic, social learning, and family-systems approaches respectively (Emery et al., 1987). One point of commonality in all three perspectives is the consideration of issues of emotional closeness and interpersonal power. These two critical aspects of interpersonal relationships are the same ones used earlier to characterize discipline styles (Maccoby & Martin, 1983), and they are the primary focus in the following overview of major individual, dyadic, and triadic issues.

Some Individual Coping Tasks

Among the major sources of internal distress in divorce are coping with the sense of loss that accompanies the marital dissolution and redefining oneself in terms of the family changes that have occurred (Hodges, 1986; Kressel, 1985; Wallerstein, 1983). Coping with the emotional loss can involve a process not unlike grieving after death, and doubts about self-efficacy can be substantial, since individual identity is often tied to family identity.

As noted in Chapter 5, the distress caused by separation or loss is greater when attachments are stronger, the terms of separation more ambiguous, and substitute attachment figures less readily available. This is true not only for children who are separated from parents, but also for adults separated from mates. Greater emotional commitment to one's spouse, more uncertainty about the possibility of reconciliation, and the absence of social support—all increase the separation distress experienced by divorcing adults. In coping with this distress, cyclical feelings of love, anger, and sadness are prominent, and, to varying degrees, their interchange is adaptive in the short-term. A major task for eventual acceptance of the new circumstances is the integration of these apparently discrepant feelings.

With regard to self-efficacy, the more strongly the definition of self is tied to family roles, the more difficult the changes introduced by divorce will be. Again, this is true for adults as well as children. For example, redefinition of self may be particularly difficult for women whose primary role identities had been as wife, mother, and homemaker. In such cases, the tasks for change involve self-acceptance and the structuring of new identities. While emotional and cognitive changes are important, ultimately the assumption of new roles inside and outside the family is most basic to the redefinition of self.

Boundaries in Dyadic Relationships

Since internal distress in divorce stems from changes in relationships, the above concerns clearly are interpersonal as well as intrapsychic. The negotiation of new interpersonal boundaries, that is, the redefinition of the implicit and explicit rules of behavior, is perhaps the major relationship task. This is true for individuals involved in various dyadic relationships and, as discussed later, for the boundaries between these subsystems themselves.

The negotiation of new boundaries takes time because their behavioral definitions are more important than their verbal ones. Moreover, it is an inherently stressful process. Lack of clarity in the rules that govern behavior is distressing in itself and also makes conflict likely, since family members are apt to violate each other's expectations. To give a concrete example, unscheduled visits may suit a nonresidential parent who wants spontaneity in his or her relationships with the children, but such visits may be viewed as intrusive by a residential parent who does not want to be constantly prepared to face a former spouse. Moreover, the uncertainty may create anxiety in a child for whom knowing when the next contact will be is reassuring, and it may be disruptive to older children who have their own plans to make.

One major task for the divorced family is the clarification of such interpersonal boundaries, regardless of their specific definition. To continue with the above example, the terms of a visitation agreement are one explicit way of defining some rules for relationships. Other implicit rules may also develop, such as honking the car horn for the children rather than coming to the door when they are picked up for a visit. For some families such rules can minimize tension and avoid potential conflict. The specifics of such boundaries may not be ideal in anyone's eyes, but at least they clarify expectations and thereby avoid some anxiety and conflict.

While the process itself is important to understand, so is the eventual definition of some interpersonal boundaries. This is particularly true with regard to the emotional distances that will be maintained and to the negotiation of relative interpersonal power. Each of these presents difficult, often painful, challenges, and the boundaries of these more abstract aspects of relationships often defy explicit definition.

Parent-child relationships. As the evidence reviewed in Chapter 5 indicated, the relationships between each parent and the children need to be redefined after divorce. Negotiation of a new emotional distance between the children and the nonresidential parent is the most salient of these changes, as data on the quantity and quality of contact indicate. Both the lack of clarity of the boundaries of this relationship and the long-term consequences of the new emotional distance are of potential concern. Erratic visitation, particularly when a parent fails to make scheduled visits, can be especially distressing, because the relationship as defined by such behavior may not match children's initial emotional and cognitive definitions of it. While children's expectations will become consistent with the behavioral terms of the relationship over time, the amount of contact and closeness maintained can be of considerable symbolic importance to children, even if evidence fails to indicate that it greatly influences their overall adjustment (see Chapter 5).

Although less prominent, the emotional distance between the residential parent and children may also be redefined following divorce. Children are likely to need extra reassurance of their parents' love, and this need comes just when the residential parent typically has many competing demands. Thus, some normal strains must be expected. As discussed in Chapter 5, both dependency upon and rejection of children are long-term problems that occasionally arise. Since this relationship is more prominent than that with the nonresidential parent, such changes have the potential for a marked impact on children.

In addition to trying to meet their emotional needs, residential parents initially may encounter difficulties in disciplining the children because of emotional and practical concerns, misattributions regarding the reasons for misbehavior, or past reliance on the other parent as the disciplinarian. Nonresidential parents may also lose authority over their children, but for different reasons. Their legitimacy may be undermined by their infrequent contact with the children, or they may view visitation as a time for fun not discipline. As discussed earlier, although there are a wide range of "healthy" parenting styles, authoritative parents who eventually learn to provide both love and discipline seem to be the most successful.

Parent-parent subsystem. For many divorcing families, the central dyadic relationship that must be redefined is the one between the divorcing parents. Ironically, having just decided that they can no longer remain married, parents must attempt to cooperate with each other over the children. This is often complicated by the discrepant emotional distances they want to set in their new relationship. The marital partners must move from being intimates to becoming friends, enemys, strangers, or associates in the "business" of child-rearing. This is especially difficult because it is unlikely that each partner wants to maintain the same emotional distance. In most divorces, one partner is more anxious to leave the relationship, and this person may have begun emotional preparation for the divorce years earlier. The partner who is left, on the other hand, usually has had less time to prepare for the divorce and may feel abandoned, rejected, and desperate. These discrepancies in emotional investment are often extremely important, especially in the first year or two after the separation. While the partner who wants to end the marriage may want to be friends, for the partner who is left the choice may be lovers or enemies.

The emotional boundary between the former spouses is central to the divorced family because it impacts not only on them but also on the parent-child-parent triad. Parents need not be "friends" to avoid triadic problems, however. Friendship, in fact, may be an impossible goal, particularly in the short-term. Rather, what is needed is agreement to cooperate with regard to the children. Thus, in divorce mediation and in family therapy, a more realistic goal is to help parents establish a businesslike relationship in which contact between them is minimal and the boundaries of the relationship are clear.

As the emotional distance between parents needs to be redefined, so does their relative power. The child-rearing authority that the parents will share or assume independently is the major concern. Here the issues range from the desire of parents to cooperate in some areas yet remain autonomous in others, to the difficulty of balancing rules in two different households, to the need for supporting each other's authority in the eyes of the children (or at least not subvert it). Potential problems with parental authority are evident most prominently in disputes about custody of the children. In addition to the physical child-care arrangements discussed in Chapter 7, a major issue that may arise in custody disputes is a symbolic one. A nonresidential parent may value the tie to the children implied by a joint-custody agreement, or a residential parent may desire the authority and responsibility connoted by the term sole custody. The identical parenting arrangement, including which decisions will be shared, where the children will reside, and what the parenting rules will be, may be viewed as either quite good or totally unacceptable according to the custody label. Partly because of these symbolic connotations, some states have dropped the term "custody" from their statutes and refer instead to "parental rights and responsibilities" (Freed & Walker, 1986).

A more practical concern about defining parental authority is determining which decisions parents will attempt to make jointly and which will be made autonomously. Again, this is an issue of boundaries. While many parents feel that decisions with regard to medical care, education, and religious training are important enough to be shared jointly, practicalities and concerns for autonomy typically necessitate considerable independence in most other areas.

Disturbances in the Parent-Child-Parent Triad

While they no longer share the same household, the parent-child-parent triad continues to influence members of the divorced family. On some occasions mother, father, and child are present together, such as major positive events like school graduations, or negative ones like custody hearings. The triad may also come together at more routine times, such as when visitation exchanges take place. Times like these can be important sources of distress or reassurance, but the greater influence of the triad comes from the boundaries that are drawn between the dyadic subsystems. Continued positive parent-child relationships may encourage the development of more positive parent-parent relationships over time, but more important is how the parent-parent relationship affects the children. Problems often develop when parents cannot separate spousal roles from parental ones.

As discussed in Chapter 5, perhaps the most basic issue related to the triad is one that concerns emotional distances, namely the loyalty dilemmas with which children are confronted. The emotional distancing that naturally takes place between partners who divorce upsets the homeostatic balance in the triad. Initially, children are likely to feel that they are being disloyal to one parent by maintaining a relationship with the other, and if parents cannot accept each other as parents, the loyalty pressures children feel can become direct and unremitting. Given this latter circumstance, children have several options. They can attempt to maintain a balanced relationship with each parent; try to improve the parents' relationship by serving as a mediator, an angel, or a scapegoat; play one parent off against the other; or withdraw physically or emotionally from both parents. On the other hand, if parents cooperate sufficiently to allow for individual parent-child relationships to develop, a new homeostastics in the triad can be found and torn loyalties resolved without such dramatic upheavals.

The parent-child-parent triad can also shape the emotional closeness of the two parent-child subsystems by influencing how the children are perceived. Both displacement and projection (intrapsychic defenses which can be reinterpreted as descriptions of interpersonal behavior) are potential sources of distortion (Emery et al., 1987). Parents can displace either positive or negative emotions felt toward their former spouse on to the children. For example, a mother may direct the hostility she feels toward her former husband on to a son who acts and perhaps looks like his father, or a father may expect a daughter to offer much of the emotional support he had previously received from his wife. Parents may also project their own feelings about a former spouse on to the children, thus distorting their perceptions of them. A parent's view that a child feels hurt, angry, or lonely may reflect more about the parent than the child.

In addition to emotional issues, disputes over parental discipline can also be disruptive to the parent-child-parent triad. Inconsistent discipline may result from unclear boundaries regarding parental authority or the lack of communication between parents. Clarification of the limits of each parent's authority and the introduction of some avenue for minimal communication can greatly help in solving these problems. Disputes over parental authority may also arise from unresolved issues of interpersonal distance or power in the parent-parent dyad, however. Thus, discipline may not just be inconsistent, but deliberately subversive. Children may be told that they need not obey the other parent, or they may be used as a conduit for communicating with or punishing the former spouse.

While many points of tension among former spouses may be

impossible to resolve, because the parent-child-parent triad often influences children's adjustment, a number of therapists advocate some type of family therapy. Presumably, intervening at the relationship level, whether from a behavioral or a systems orientation, should be more effective than individual therapy. Unfortunately, because of wide gaps in treatment-outcome research, this is little more than a presumption at the present time.

RESEARCH ON THE OUTCOME OF THERAPEUTIC INTERVENTIONS IN DIVORCE

Therapy with children from divorced families can be classified into three broad categories: individual therapy for children, family approaches, and groups. Despite the great number of techniques that have been developed in each of these formats (see Hodges, 1986), only a handful of systematic treatment-outcome studies have been conducted. Other than the observation that divorced families are particularly likely to drop out of traditional child-guidance clinics (Rembar, Novick, & Kalter, 1982), individual therapy has not been systematically studied at all. School-based groups have been evaluated in a handful of sound studies, and this research is presented at the end of this section. Family therapy is examined first. Except for divorce mediation, family interventions in divorce have only been investigated incidentally, however.

Family Intervention

In a review of outcome research on divorce therapy, Sprenkle and Storm (1983) concluded that divorce mediation was the only area of family intervention where adequate research had been conducted, and positive effects demonstrated. Divorce mediation is a new method for settling divorce disputes and shares common elements with both legal and therapeutic interventions in divorce (see Chapter 7 for a discussion of this and other legal interventions in divorce). In mediation, parents meet together with an impartial third party who attempts to help them resolve their differences cooperatively. While the goal of mediation is to negotiate a fair divorce agreement, mediators are generally aware of and have the opportunity to address the individual, dyadic, and triadic issues discussed above (Emery et al., in press).

As reviewed in Chapter 7, evidence does support mediation as a viable alternative to the adversarial settlement of divorce disputes. While it may be adequate relative to other studies of intervention in divorce, mediation research is hardly sufficient, however (Emery & Wyer, 1987a). Probably the single biggest need is further investigation of mediation as a preventive family intervention that may have beneficial psychological effects on all members of the divorced family. At present, no major effects have been demonstrated (Emery & Wyer, 1987a).

Other investigations reviewed by Sprenkle and Storm (1983) include attempts to reconcile separated spouses, court counseling programs, and education groups, but none of these studies incorporated sufficient methodological controls. Even more distressing is that, despite the widely held opinion that conjoint treatment is most appropriate for divorced families (Gurman, Kniskern, & Pinsof, 1986), *no* systematic studies of family therapy designed specifically for divorced families have been undertaken to date. However, there are two small literatures that hold some implications for family therapy in divorce: interventions with divorced adults and investigations of marital conflict or divorce as a predictor of outcome in family treatments.

One of the few systematic investigations of therapeutic interventions with divorced adults is the prevention study undertaken by Bloom, Hodges, and Caldwell (1982). In this study, recently separated adults were randomly assigned to different intervention groups that focused on one of five different topics: (a) employment problems, (b) legal and financial issues, (c) parenting concerns, (d) housing and homemaking arrangements, and (e) social and emotional well-being. A no-treatment control group was also obtained. At a six-month follow-up, the adults in the treatment groups reported less anxiety, fatigue, and increased physical well-being compared to no-treatment controls. Interestingly, the five treatment groups did not differ from each other, suggesting the general effect of group support rather than a specific effect due to the substantive topic. At a 30-month follow-up, treatment effects were even greater than at six months, and some significant treatment benefits were still found four years after the initial intervention. Although some differences due to the specific type of intervention were found at later follow-ups, the general treatment effect continued to be most notable (Bloom, Hodges, Kern, & McFaddin, 1985).

Given the psychological distress divorce causes for many adults (Bloom, Asher, & White, 1978), this research is distinctly important in its own right. Unfortunately, its implications for children's adjustment are only suggestive, since the impact of parents' functioning on the wider family system was not examined. While further research focusing on adults is clearly warranted, an important question to address is what impact, if any, improvements in the parents' functioning have on their children.

Studies of family interventions with disturbed children that have examined how marital conflict or divorce predicts treatment outcome also have some relevance to therapy with divorced families. Two findings from this literature are worth noting. First, behavioral parent training for conduct problem children can be effective even in the face of marital conflict in two-parent families. Marital discord generally does not foreshadow unsuccessful outcome immediately following treatment (Brody & Forehand, 1985; Oltmanns, Broderick, & O'Leary, 1977). In fact, improved child behavior can increase marital satisfaction, a finding consistent with a systems perspective (Brody & Forehand, 1985). The second finding indicates, however, that when treatments targeting marital distress or partner support are included, behavior therapy for children is more effective than when parent training is the sole focus. Increased effectiveness is particularly evident when the marital relationship is distressed and when longer-term follow-up measures are obtained (Dadds, Schwartz, & Sanders, 1987; Griest et al., 1982; Margolin & Christensen, 1981; Webster-Stratton, 1985).

These findings indicate that the involvement of the nonresidential parent may be helpful in interventions with divorced families, especially when parental conflict is linked to the child's problems or the residential parent is in need of support. Frequent conjoint sessions may be inappropriate in many such circumstances, but parenting plans can be arranged in occasional joint meetings or through individual appointments. When support from the nonresidential parent is absent or unlikely, clinicians should help residential parents to identify other sources of parenting support. Unless alternative supports are developed, isolated parents are particularly apt to become dependent on a therapist and to fail to maintain treatment gains (Wahler, 1980).

School-Based Groups

School-based groups for children of divorce have been the subject of several uncontrolled evaluations, as well as a few controlled studies (see Pedro-Carroll & Cowen, in press). Most of the studies have been preventive interventions in which the treated children were not specifically identified as requiring help. Given the fact that the children were functioning adequately beforehand, it is impressive that some beneficial outcomes have been demonstrated.

The most thorough study conducted to date is Pedro-Carroll's Children of Divorce Project (CODIP), an outgrowth of Cowen's well-known series of investigations on school-based preventive interventions (Pedro-Carroll & Cowen, in press). In this project, a 12-session divorce support group was offered to 4th to 6th grade boys and girls. The groups had the goals of providing an opportunity for divorced children to share their experiences and of teaching specific skills related to interpersonal problem-solving, communication, and the expression of anger.

In a comparison of treated and demographically-matched untreated children, statistically significant improvements in teachers' ratings of problems and competencies were found for CODIP children. In addition, parents reported improved communication with their children, and significant decreases in anxiety were reported by the children themselves (Pedro-Carroll & Cowen, 1985). Similar improvements were found in a replication study (Pedro-Carroll, Cowen, Hightower, & Guare, 1986).

Stolberg's Divorce Adjustment Project, an intervention program which was the initial model for the CODIP, also provides some support for the effectiveness of school-based groups. Four groups were compared in this investigation: (a) a children's support group, (b) a single-parents' support group, (c) a group in which children and parents participated in their respective groups, and (d) a no-treatment control group. Based on either posttreatment or five-month follow-up evaluations, data indicated that the support group improved children's self-esteem and social skills compared to the untreated controls, and the parents' support group prevented deterioration in their adjustment to divorce relative to the no-treatment group. When the children's group was run concurrently with a parents' group, however, no improvements over controls were found for either children or parents (Stolberg & Anker, 1984; Stolberg, Cullen, & Garrison, 1982; Stolberg & Garrison, 1985). Demographic differences may have accounted for this last finding, since the parents in the combined group had been separated longer, had less adequate jobs, and reported less involvement on the part of the noncustodial parent (Stolberg & Garrison, 1985).

The results of these two projects, together with the reports of more informal program evaluations (Pedro-Carroll & Cowen, in press), provide some optimistic evidence for the effectiveness of school-based support groups. Apparently the opportunity to share concerns with peers, together with the mastery of specific skills for dealing with divorce, can be helpful to children as well as adults.

SUMMARY

In this chapter, evidence on family processes in divorce has been examined from a more clinical perspective. Potential individual and relationship problems with regard to emotional closeness and interpersonal power were highlighted. At the individual level, the two major issues identified were coping with the sense of loss and redefining one's own identity in light of changes in family identity. At the dyadic level, the stress and conflict involved in negotiating new interpersonal boundaries were highlighted, especially with regard to the parents' relationship. Discrepancies in the partners' desires for closeness in their relationship and the need to define parental authority are two of the major obstacles confronted by former spouses who remain parents. Finally, ways in which the parent-child-parent triad continue to influence members of divorced families were discussed. The separation of the parents' past and present relationship with each other from their individual relationships with the children is most important in establishing a new homeostasis in this triad.

The small body of research on treatment outcome was also examined in this chapter. There is some evidence to suggest that family therapies are more effective than individual ones, and the idea that divorced children benefit from school-based support groups has received some empirical support. The biggest conclusion from this review, however, is that more treatment-outcome research is sorely needed.

Having moved from a very broad to an increasingly specific focus on marriage, divorce, and children in the first six chapters, a wider perspective is adopted again in the last chapter, wherein social policy is examined.

7

INTERVENING IN DIVORCE: LEGAL POLICIES

If studies on psychotherapy are few, those on the effectiveness of legal interventions with divorced families are scarce. This is unfortunate since a variety of legal policies have been designed to influence divorce and its consequences. While the absence of research limits the conclusions that can be reached about its effects, the goals of legal interventions can be examined in the light of the empirical findings reviewed in Chapters 4 and 5. Since policies are designed for the "average" family, the group research from these chapters is particularly relevant. Thus, it is possible to evaluate the objectives of interventions in divorce, if not their effectiveness.

Three general topics are discussed in the present overview of legal policies, beginning with the state's role in regulating divorce. The central issues here are changes in the acceptable grounds for granting a divorce, and questions about whether the state should or should not discourage divorce by making it difficult to obtain. The second topic concerns divorce settlements and related efforts to provide economic and parenting support to children from divorced families. Child custody, visitation, and the economic obligations of divorced parents to each other and their children are the issues examined. Finally, the process by which divorce settlements are reached is considered. The settlement of disputes in the adversary system is one focus, and a new means of resolving differences, divorce mediation, is the other.

In reviewing these topics, some attention is paid to historical developments, current practices, and future directions. This approach is designed to convey a sense of the direction many new developments in family law are taking. It is also intended to indicate a sense of diversity, because divorce laws differ from state to state. One state's history is sometimes another state's current practice; one state's current practice may be another state's future.

LEGAL REGULATION OF DIVORCE

Until the twentieth century, the primary goal of divorce law was to uphold marriage by making divorce difficult (Halem, 1981). In Europe, the Catholic church controlled marriage until the Reformation, and rarely allowed couples to divorce. Although broadened somewhat under civil regulation, few actions were deemed sufficient grounds for divorce, and its low incidence through the nineteenth century speaks of the deterrent effect of the regulations (Halem, 1981).

The activist approach that characterized religious and civil regulation of divorce for hundreds of years seems to have been replaced with a more reactive policy during the 1900s. Faced with the practical problem of deciding an ever-increasing number of divorce actions, the judiciary slowly accommodated changing social attitudes through increasingly broader interpretations of the grounds for divorce (Plateris, 1974).

While judicial practice changed gradually over many years, legislative policy has been altered much more recently and much more dramatically. The most important change has been the widespread passage of no-fault divorce laws, first enacted in California in 1970 and since passed by all 50 states (Freed & Walker, 1986). A no-fault divorce is granted when both spouses request it and, in some states, the request of only one partner suffices. The only major requirement is that a fixed waiting period be observed, a time which may be lengthier if children are involved or if one partner does not want to end the marriage. Although some states have retained fault divorce as an option, the majority of couples in these states file no-fault actions (Freed & Walker, 1986).

The passage of no-fault divorce laws represents a substantial move toward the deregulation of divorce. Whereas laws were once explicitly designed to discourage marital dissolution, divorce has become essentially a private decision. The tremendous significance of this change should not be overlooked. In the eyes of the law, divorce, like marriage, is now a matter of individual choice. In some cultures, marital partners are not allowed to chose their own mates, let alone to end their marriage.

The introduction of no-fault divorce was a reaction to broad social changes, but it was also designed to achieve some specific legal goals. One was to eliminate collusion between married partners to prove to the court that they had sufficient grounds to divorce, a situation which often led to perjury. Another was to remove acrimony from the legal proceedings, as fault divorces could be terribly divisive (Weitzman, 1985). More generally, no-fault divorce is part of a broader attempt in contemporary law to accommodate an increasingly pluralistic society. As the social consensus that the state *should* discourage divorce has been questioned, at least by some, increasingly neutral regulations have had to be enacted in order to avoid imposing values on members of a diverse society. Hence there has been a movement away from regulating divorce and other family matters, allowing individual families and family members to determine the nature of their own relationships (Schneider, 1985).

Disincentives to Divorce and Incentives to Remain Married

No-fault divorce represents the explicit removal of one attempt to regulate divorce. Still, two points are essential to note. First, no-fault laws cannot be blamed for the current high rate of divorce. As noted in Chapter 2, the divorce rate has risen gradually over the last 100 years, and the introduction of no-fault laws in various states was *not* followed by a dramatic increase in divorce. Second, no-fault divorce notwithstanding, significant disincentives to divorce do remain. Its economic consequences are one such disincentive, as demonstrated in the income-maintenance experiments. Similarly, the fact that married couples with young children are less likely to divorce indicates that the presence of children serves as a disincentive to divorce, or more optimistically, as an incentive to remain married. In fact, all of the adverse consequences detailed in earlier chapters can be construed as disincentives to divorce.

Despite these naturalistic disincentives, some are concerned that no-fault divorce is a retreat from moral discourse in family law (Schneider, 1985), and others have suggested that the adverse consequences of divorce for children provide justification for making divorce more difficult to obtain. Each view, however, can be challenged on empirical, as well as ideological, grounds. Increases in divorce rates appear to be a result of changing social and economic conditions, not just a retreat from morality (although the accommodation of pluralism has clearly made it more difficult for state legislatures to articulate a moral code, a consequence many do not bemoan). Moreover, family processes that are not inevitable consequences of divorce appear to be the primary cause of distress for children from divorced families (although divorce often does increase problems in family relationships). Finally, the literature of the recent past indicates that the problems attributed to no-fault divorce existed in the fault-based system, along with a series of additional difficulties.

Broadly speaking, making divorce more difficult seems to be an indirect and negatively focused way of preserving marriage and the care of children. If marriage is to be safeguarded, creating incentives to remain married would seem to be a more positive approach than creating disincentives to divorce. As for children, a potentially more fruitful tactic would be to develop policies that ensure the fulfillment of *parental* responsibilities by adults, be those responsibilities psychological, social, or economic, and whether they be fulfilled inside or outside marriage. The disputes that often arise in divorce outline some of those parental responsibilities.

DIVORCE SETTLEMENTS

Five areas of potential dispute may require some form of legal intervention in divorce. Three of these issues pertain to financial matters: the division of property, the allocation of spousal support, and the assignment of child support. The other two issues, custody and visitation, concern child-rearing. Of course, divorced parents must negotiate many other issues, either together or independently, but the courts generally limit themselves to the five issues listed here.

Ironically, as the state's role in regulating divorce has diminished, the courts have become increasingly involved in determining divorce settlements. This is due both to demographic changes and to vague standards for deciding divorce settlements, which encourage divorcing spouses to litigate. Like the laws specifying the grounds for divorce, the rules governing financial and child-care settlements have been made more general in order to accommodate a diversity of families. In some cases, legislation does little more than impel judges to make good and fair decisions, thus putting an incredible amount of discretion in the hands of individual trial judges. While, in theory, this gives the judiciary flexibility in responding to individual families, in practice, it has given rise to a number of undesirable consequences. Litigation is encouraged because the outcomes of court hearings are often unpredictable; acrimony is increased because virtually any evidence that makes one partner look bad and the other look good may be deemed to be relevant to the proceedings; the potential for bias on the part of individual judges is increased; and appellate review is limited because there are few criteria for evaluating the exercise of judicial discretion (Mnookin, 1975). Finally, many divorced adults feel that they are treated unfairly because the state's conception of the marriage contract, as communicated by the terms of the divorce settlement, does not match their own.

Legal policies governing divorce settlements are considered below in relation to this global increase in indeterminate standards and to specific developments in financial and child-care settlements.

Financial Settlements and Postdivorce Economics

Family expenses increase following divorce, in part, because two households are more expensive to maintain than one. But, as discussed in Chapter 5, it has been convincingly documented that divorced mothers and their custodial children suffer more economically than divorced fathers. This fact is partly explained by the financial settlements that are negotiated at the time of divorce and the poor compliance with those settlements. Another, more general reason, however, involves differences in the employment and compensation of men and women.

With regard to divorce settlements, property division, spousal support (alimony), and child support are all potential ways of reallocating finances between former spouses. Each deserves at least brief consideration.

Property division. Property division concerns the allocation of the assets brought to or acquired during the marriage. While it is often assumed that the property of the marriage should be divided into roughly equal amounts, except in a few states, judges determine property awards individually (and hence the concerns raised about the exercise of discretion apply here). In addition, three important changes that affect property distribution should be noted: the property that each spouse brought to, or acquired during, the marriage is increasingly being viewed as belonging to both parties, the definition of property is expanding, and fault has become less of a consideration in dividing property.

With the exception of a handful of "community property" states where assets have always been assumed to be owned jointly, historically a couple's property was deemed to belong to whoever held the legal title to it. Under these provisions, the courts had to award property according to its title, dividing only jointly held assets upon divorce. This created inequitable situations when, for various reasons, only one spouse was listed as the sole owner of marital assets, such as a business, investments, or the family home. Recent laws have changed this situation, however, allowing for the "equitable distribution" of marital property irrespective of title. As of 1985, all states except Arizona, Mississippi, and South Carolina had either community property or equitable distribution statutes, thus giving each spouse ownership of the property acquired during the marriage and, in some cases, to all of each other's property including premarital holdings and inheritances, in the absence of a prenuptial agreement (Freed & Walker, 1986).

The expanding definition of marital property is another important change in divorce law. Most state statutes now recognize nonmonetary contributions to the marriage, such as homemaker and parental responsibilities, as being important to the acquisition of marital property (Freed & Walker, 1986), and many state courts have recognized nontangible assets, such as pension plans, business goodwill, professional education, and insurance policies to be a part of the property to be divided upon divorce (Weitzman, 1985). Thus, for example, when one spouse works to put another through professional school and the couple divorces shortly thereafter, in some states the value of the professional education is considered to be a part of their marital property.

As in other areas of divorce law, fault is of diminishng importance in determining property settlements. Although once a major consideration, fault has largely been reduced to a "bargaining chip" that may help achieve, but does not require, a more favorable settlement for the spouse who is not at fault. In 1985, 21 states specifically excluded fault from consideration in property division, 20 allowed but did not require it to be considered, and the remainder did not address the issue (Freed & Walker, 1986).

As fault considerations continue to erode, a clear articulation is needed of what assets constitute marital property (e.g., pension plans but not future earning power). Furthermore, the adoption of a rule that would divide property equally rather than equitably would clarify policy and limit judicial discretion, and might also lead to improved settlements for women (Weitzman, 1985). While such rules might increase fairness in individual settlements, unfortunately these changes in property law cannot have a major influence on the average economic situation of custodial mothers and their children. The reason for this is that most divorcing couples have few fixed assets to divide (Weitzman, 1985).

There is, however, one area of property division that could have an important and immediate impact on children: the disposition of the family home. The home is usually the most valuable marital asset and is often sold to facilitate property division. In one study an explicit order to sell the family home to facilitate property division was found in one out of every three cases (Weitzman, 1985). Given all the changes that children encounter at the time of divorce, it seems desirable that this source of stability be maintained. While many couples negotiate property settlements that allow children to remain in the marital home, many state laws contain no provisions to encourage this arrangement. Perhaps what is needed is legislation that states a preference against selling the family home until the children reach the age of majority, the residential parent remarries, or the partners agree otherwise. Each parent could maintain partial ownership of the home, with the nonresidential parent continuing to contribute to mortgage and upkeep expenses, both as a way of providing child support and of protecting his/her investment.

Spousal support. If the small amount of marital property limits how much it can be used to balance the postdivorce living standards of men and women, the payment of spousal support (alimony) is unlikely to provide the solution either. With the increase in two-earner households, changing conceptions of men's and women's roles, and the movement away from fault divorce, the rationales for one spouse supporting the other are disappearing. Moreover, the proportion of divorced women awarded alimony has always been much smaller than is publicly perceived. For example, census data indicate that, among divorced women surveyed in 1981, only 14% received alimony (U.S. Census Bureau, 1983).

Women who have been married longer are much more likely to receive spousal support; however, the trend appears to be to limit its duration. Awards for "rehabilitative" alimony, in which support is provided for a fixed time, are increasing, at least in California

(Weitzman, 1985). This temporary support is designed to give the recipient an opportunity to improve his or her earning power. Such awards recognize that individuals may choose to pursue homemaker roles over worker roles in a marriage, but they suggest that divorce closes out that option.

In general, alimony is an unlikely avenue for significant policy change. Perhaps the most important conclusion is that people who choose family roles over employment options need to recognize the possible consequences of this choice.

Child support. Child support has received the most attention with respect to the redistribution of postdivorce family income. Increasing child-support awards, and in particular improving compliance with awards as ordered, has been the target of a number of state and federal efforts (NICSE, 1986). Child support is a fruitful area for policy initiatives because settlements can be based on future earning power rather than the value of fixed assets and, unlike the reasons used to justify alimony, the rationales for supporting one's children have not been questioned. In general, child-support policies focus on parental, not marital, responsibilities—an approach that should be encouraged in other areas.

Three broad issues present problems for the child-support solution, however. First, compliance with child-support awards is notoriously bad. Second, there is no widely accepted means of determining how much child support should be awarded. Third, one cannot improve the economic situation of children without improving that of their residential parents.

In 1981, 59% of all the single mothers with children had been ordered to receive child support, but only 47% of all awards were paid as ordered. In 28% of the cases, not a single payment was made (NICSE, 1986). This tremendous enforcement problem has been attacked aggressively by policy makers, who are concerned with the number of single mothers who receive AFDC. Simply put, the push is to "get tough" with fathers who fail to pay child support. As an incentive for stringent enforcement, federal legislation enacted in 1984 provides money for administrative expenses for enforcement programs, and allows the states to keep a portion of their collections of child-support payments for AFDC recipients. Among the mechanisms that can be used to insure compliance are the garnishment of wages, interception of tax refunds, and civil or criminal contempt proceedings (NICSE, 1986). Evidence indicates that such measures are effective, as collections have increased substantially in the last several years. Nevertheless, stringent enforcement policies—including the incarceration of those who fail to pay support—are most effective when they are self-starting (Chambers, 1979). In self-starting systems, state agencies assume the burden of initiating action when payments are delinquent. This automatic pursuit is preferred over leaving the matter to custodial parents who may find it too complicated, emotionally trying, or expensive to seek compliance with court-ordered awards on their own.

While enforcement is a problem for which solutions are beginning to be pursued, there is little consensus as to how much child support should be awarded. What is needed is a clear formula that takes into account each parent's income, the children's needs, and factors such as inflation. Despite a great number of proposed formulas, none has been widely accepted. Some states do offer guidelines on appropriate payment levels, and the 1984 federal child support legislation requires all states to have some schedule in place in 1987 (NICSE, 1986). Greater acceptance of such schedules is of considerable potential benefit, both as a means of removing acrimony from debates about appropriate awards and as a way of further institutionalizing the payment of support obligations. In this regard, an example of a very straightforward program is the one that has been implemented in Wisconsin. A wage-withholding on father's income is required, so that 17% is withheld for one child, 25% for two, 29% for three, 31% for four, and 35% for five or more children. While the percentages may seem arbitrary, by way of comparison the average combined child support and alimony awards rarely exceed one-third of net income in states with less explicit rules (Weitzman, 1985).

The last problem in child support is the toughest. In order to support a child at a higher standard of living, the residential parent must share that standard. Mothers have custody of their children in the vast majority of cases, however, and, on the average, women earn substantially less than men. Thus, in order to balance the living standards of children and their noncustodial fathers, a sum of money considerably greater than that associated with the added expense of raising children would have to be transferred. This leads to a consideration of the broader financial situation of custodial mothers.

Postdivorce economics for single mothers. Equity in the allocation of property, spousal support, and child support is important in its own right, and financial settlements can improve the economic situation of children. These methods of transfer make up only a small percentage of the income of single-mother families, however. In the year following divorce, 60% of the income in single-mother families comes from the women's own labor, and 10% from the combination of alimony and child support. Even among the group receiving the highest average payments—white women with postdivorce incomes above the median—the combination of alimony and child support accounts for only 20% of their average postdivorce income (Duncan & Hoffman, 1985).

Certainly, there are individual cases where alimony and/or child support payments contribute substantially greater amounts. Moreover, the supplemental income coming from these awards is important, even if it is proportionally small. Nevertheless, these data indicate that, unless a drastic departure from current practices is entertained, one must look beyond the terms of divorce settlements to eliminate the economic hardships experienced by mothers and their custodial children. Three potential solutions are apparent: improved employment, public assistance, and remarriage.

Women clearly attempt to raise their family income by increasing their employment following divorce. In the Michigan Panel Study of Income Dynamics it was found that whereas 51% women reported working over 1,000 hours in the year prior to divorce, 72% did so in the first year afterwards (Duncan & Hoffman, 1985). The percentage of women who received over $250 in public assistance during this period also increased from 5.0% to 19%. Nevertheless, their incomes fell well below predivorce levels. In the first year following divorce, the average income of women who did not remarry dropped from $26,000 to less than $15,000 (in 1981 dollars). In this first year, men also experienced a drop in income to 93% of the predivorce level, compared with a 17% increase for couples who remained married. However, men's total incomes, and especially their incomes relative to their family needs, do not suffer as much and rebound more quickly than do women's (Duncan & Hoffman, 1985). Obviously, any general improvement in the job outlook for women would improve the status of single mothers.

Women who enter or re-enter the workforce after divorce have sacrificed earning potential by assuming the homemaker role. For them, it might be hoped that the increased experience or retraining opportunities that come with time will improve their economic situation. Indeed, this possibility is a major rationale behind the "rehabilitative alimony" awards discussed above. While retraining and increased experience will certainly help some, on the average time makes little difference. Five years after divorce, men's family income has increased 23% over predivorce levels, and their income relative to their needs by 29%. But, with one subgroup excluded, women's income stubbornly remains about 30% below predivorce levels, with income relative to needs about 10% below predivorce levels (Duncan & Hoffman, 1985).

The subgroup excluded from the above statistics comprises women who remarry. More than any other single factor, remarriage relieves the economic distress of divorced women. Five years after divorce the incomes of remarried women are 27% *above* predivorce levels and income relative to needs is up 25%—figures comparable to those for divorced men and couples who remain married. Without doubt, there are strong economic incentives to remarry and, while encouraging remarriage may not be an intentional policy, it is a de facto one. The economic situation of divorced women (among other factors) encourages remarriage, and the relatively low financial obligations of men to their first families allows them to support a second one.

Custody, Visitation, Postdivorce Parenting

The major parenting determination in divorce settlements is who will have custody of the children. This question encompasses decisions both about children's primary residence and about who will have the authority to make child-care decisions. A secondary determination is how often noncustodial parents will be allowed to "visit" with their children. Partly as a result of difficulties in arriving at these decisions, some recent legal interventions in custody/visitation reflect an increasing concern for enhancing the quality of postdivorce family relationships, rather than simply determining the quantity of contact to be allowed.

Rules for determining sole custody. Child-custody standards constitute a prime example of the vagueness characterizing divorce laws, and the problems that accompany indeterminacy. According to current practice, custody is awarded in accordance with the future "best interests" of the children involved. In addition to sharing problems with other indeterminate rules, it has been noted that the "best interests" standard is complicated by these facts: (a) psychologists have not demonstrated an ability to reliably predict the future development of individual children, and, (b) even if reliable prediction were possible, the potential debates about what alternative futures are "best" are unending (Mnookin, 1975).

While most state statutes contain guidelines for determining children's best interests (Freed & Walker, 1986), these too are very general. For example, judges may be urged to consider such factors as the capacity of the parents to give love to the children, to care for their material needs, the stability of the family home, and the mental and physical health of all the parties involved. Since those cases that come before a judge are the ones in which there is not a clear preference for one parent over the other, such vague considerations offer little guidance as to how judicial discretion should be exercised.

Custody rules were not always so general. For the greater part of history, fathers automatically received custody of their children. Roman law gave men total control over their children (and their wives), and this authority changed little through the Middle Ages (Derdeyn, 1976). By the nineteenth century, men's absolute control over their families had diminished in the eyes of the law, but judicial decisions continued to reflect fathers' superior right to custody.

A new standard—the tender years presumption—emerged during the nineteenth century, and initiated a shift in custodial preference from fathers to mothers. According to this doctrine, children of "tender years" were considered best cared for by their mothers. Through the twentieth century, the age range thought to constitute the "tender years" gradually expanded from infancy to include adolescence. By the 1960s, the presumption of father custody based on paternal rights, had been replaced by the presumption favoring mother custody, based on the best interests of the child (Weiss, 1979b).

The current "best interests" standard was actually established in the early twentieth century as part of the *parens patriae* role of juvenile courts, but the "tender years" presumption strongly directed judicial determinations about what was in the child's best interests until the 1970s. The women's movement, new ideas about parental roles for men and women, and questions of sex bias subsequently raised serious questions about the tender years presumption. This has led to its virtual elimination from statutory law, and other influences on custody determinations, such as the finding of fault, have undergone a similar decline (Freed & Walker, 1986). The convergence of these historical developments makes the "best interests" standard so vague that it offers very little guidance to judges on how to exercise their discretion.

While there is little legislative guidance, historical factors surely influence the exercise of judicial discretion implicitly, if not explicitly. For example, a survey of California judges indicated that 85% still reported a preference for maternal custody despite the passage of gender-neutral custody legislation (Weitzman, 1985).

Joint-custody. The traditional rules for determining custody assume that one or the other parent must be awarded sole custody upon separation or divorce. To put it more accurately, the assumption has been that one parent must *lose* custody, since both have equal rights and responsibilities in marriage. As a way out of this assumption and the dilemma created by the indeterminate sole-custody standards, it has been suggested that both parents should retain custody of their children upon divorce. Joint custody has also been said to be beneficial to children. As of 1985, 32 states had statutes which allowed or encouraged joint custody, and evidence indicates that joint-custody awards are on the increase (Freed & Walker, 1986).

While joint-custody has been widely promoted in a very short period of time, a number of controversies have been engendered by this trend. Specific issues include concerns such as, how or whether joint-custody should affect child-support payments, and whether geographic mobility can be restricted when divorced parents have joint-custody (see Folberg, 1984). While these and other issues will need to be addressed as the trend increases, the most important current debates center around one of two controversies about whether or not joint-custody should be encouraged in the first place.

The first debate concerns differences between joint legal and joint physical custody. In joint *legal* custody, parental rights and responsibilities (decision making) are shared, but the children spend a considerably greater portion of their time with one parent. In joint *physical* custody, not only is legal guardianship shared, but children also spend approximately the same amount of time with each parent. While it has opponents, joint legal custody is generally viewed more favorably that joint physical custody. Some joint-custody proponents, on the other hand, believe that the only true joint-custody arrangement is joint physical custody (Folberg, 1984).

The second major debate revolves around the extent to which joint-custody should be encouraged. The full gamut of options has been proposed: joint-custody should not be allowed; it should be allowed only when parents elect it; or it should be the preferred option, one that a judge can order even over the objections of one or both parents (Folberg, 1984; Scott & Derdeyn, 1984). While most state laws simply define the term and allow it to be an option, some states indicate a preference or a presumption in favor of joint-custody (a presumption is stronger than a preference), and some allow judges to make joint-custody awards even against the parents' wishes. Others contain "friendly parent" rules designed to encourage parents to elect joint-custody. Under these provisions, should a sole-custody award be made, the parent who will most strongly encourage contact between the children and the noncustodial parent is favored (Folberg, 1984).

Typically, state statutes are silent on whether joint physical custody is to be encouraged in addition to joint legal custody, leaving the matter to judicial discretion. Recent evidence on divorce settlements in California indicates that while joint physical-custody awards may be increasing to some extent, increases in joint legal custody are much greater. In fact, many joint legal-custody agreements strongly resemble sole-custody and visitation agreements in terms of residential arrangements (Maccoby & Mnookin, 1986).

While strong joint-custody statutes solve the problems that indeterminate sole-custody standards create for judges, clearcut sole-custody rules would have the same effect. Therefore, another rationale behind the joint-custody movement must be considered: that it will lead to better psychological adjustment among children. As discussed in Chapter 5, evidence in support of this assertion is not overwhelming. Some benefits have been found to accrue and the promotion of more positive relationships between all members of the divorced family is an important goal, but relationships have not been found to differ as dramatically as had been hoped under joint- and sole-custody arrangements. Since most of the families studied to date freely elected joint-custody, this tentative support for joint-custody is weakened further, undermining it as a solution to the indeterminacy problem. Since judicial decisions need to be made only when parents cannot agree, a preference for awarding joint-custody in contested cases may be targeting the right solution at the wrong group of parents (Scott & Derdeyn, 1984). On the other hand, there is little evidence to support the opposite claim—that joint-custody is harmful to children—and few oppose joint-custody for parents who elect the option. In fact, as a protection against potential judicial opposition, some statutes include a presumption that joint-custody is in the children's best interests when parents elect it (Folberg, 1984).

In general, we are reminded that parenting, not legal-custody status, is the real issue in terms of facilitating children's adjustment to divorce. While joint-custody laws may eventually help to change attitudes about the need for cooperation in parenting there seem to be limits to what can be achieved currently. Perhaps what is needed is a legal presumption that parental rights and responsibilities will continue to be shared jointly upon separation/divorce, unless or until the matter is contested before a judge. At this point, the presumption would shift to one of sole custody, with no further attempt to coerce cooperation with "friendly parent" or related rules.

Finally, because of the variety of physical child-care possibilities that may be arranged, the desire to interfere minimally in the family, and the need for parents to be aware of potential problems in post-divorce parenting, perhaps the best policy in regard to physical custody is to educate parents so that they can determine the arrangements that will suit them best. Part of this education may take place in mediation, as discussed below, or it could be conducted by mental health professionals, as mentioned in Chapter 6.

Since explicit rules for determining custody in contested cases are not likely to receive general acceptance quickly, and because custody contests themselves can be contrary to children's best interests, various means of encouraging private settlement, such as divorce mediation, have been promoted.

SETTLEMENT OF DIVORCE DISPUTES

The above discussion focused on the content of custody settlements. An overview of legal intervention in divorce would be incomplete without mention of the process by which divorce disputes are settled. This is particularly necessary since, in the absence of clearcut substantive guidelines, a number of procedural reforms have been attempted.

New Actors in Adversary Procedures

One set of new procedures has introduced additional actors into custody hearings, namely, attorneys, mental-health professionals, and the children themselves. In addition to lawyers for the mother and for the father, with increasing frequency attorneys have been appointed specifically to represent the children's interests in custody disputes. Evidence indicates that *guardians ad litem*, as these lawyers are often called, feel that their role is a useful one, and judges apparently rely heavily on their input (Landsman & Minow, 1978). There is some debate, however, as to whether a guardian should function as a third legal adversary, who advocates for the child's wishes, or as an independent fact-finder/mediator. Moreover, if the latter role is preferred, there is additional controversy as to whether lawyers or mental-health professionals are best trained to serve in this intermediary role (Landsman & Minow, 1978).

In addition to serving as guardians in some states, mental-health professionals have become more involved in custody hearings by conducting evaluations of children and their parents and recommending to the court more or less desirable custody dispositions. When appointed as a representative of the court, the evaluator can exercise considerable leverage, and he or she may serve some of the same fact-finder/mediator functions fulfilled by the guardian. On the other hand, expert witnesses who testify on the part of one parent can be expected to be countered by the other parent's expert. Such a "battle of the experts" can introduce rather than reduce confusion in the procedures. Furthermore, as noted earlier, there is little evidence that mental-health professionals can predict children's futures reliably, despite the apparent willingness of some to do so.

There has also been some attempt to involve children to a greater extent in custody decisions by soliciting their preferences directly or indirectly and giving them weight in court. While there is a certain intuitive appeal to having children participate in a decision about their own future best interests, on closer consideration encouraging their formal participation may be exactly the wrong approach (Emery, 1987). If being caught in the middle of their parents' conflicts in one of the greatest sources of distress for children, then soliciting their opinion as to who is their preferred custodian is hardly a solution. The articulation of a preference can be tantamount to asking children to choose between their parents, a choice which is hardly a solution to their torn loyalties. While the wishes of older children must be carefully considered in some custody determinations, children in such circumstances are likely to make their wishes known, and at least one parent will be highly motivated to communicate these desires to the court. In cases where preferences are not so clearcut, when children are asked who they want to live with, the message would seem to be: "Your parents cannot decide, nor can the judge, the guardian, nor the mental-health professional. You tell us what to do."

Divorce Mediation

A second, more sweeping, set of procedural reforms has attempted to completely circumvent the adversarial settlement of divorce disputes. As part of the movement toward the de-legalization of divorce and in response to concerns that adversarial approaches only serve to exacerbate conflict, there has been tremendous recent interest in pursuing alternative means of resolving divorce disputes. In particular, divorce mediation has been advanced as a promising alternative (Emery & Wyer, 1987a).

About 90% of all divorce disputes are settled outside court in negotiations conducted by the spouses' attorneys. However, the ever-present backdrop of the court hearing—the "shadow of law" (Mnookin & Kornhauser, 1979)—can make these negotiations highly acrimonious. In addition, while hearings at the time of divorce are relatively rare, a third or more of all parents appear in court at some time subsequent to their divorce in a dispute concerning their children (Foster & Freed, 1973–74). Whether an agreement is reached outside court or in a court hearing, concerns have been raised that the adversary system increases rather than resolves pre-existing family tensions. Dissatisfaction with the adversarial settlement of divorce disputes has been expressed by judges (Burger, 1982), lawyers (McHenry, Herrman, & Weber, 1978), and divorced spouses themselves (Spanier & Anderson, 1979).

Mediation is a form of dispute resolution that seems more consistent with the view of divorce as a process of reorganizing the family system (Jacobs, 1986). In mediation, both parents meet together with a single professional whose goal is to help them identify areas of dispute and to negotiate mutually acceptable settlements. Since mediation is based on the assumption of parental cooperation, the process is thought to have the potential to have beneficial effects on parents' and children's future relationships. Since parents make their own decisions in mediation, it is also consistent with the movement toward the private ordering of divorce (Emery & Wyer, 1987a).

Because divorce mediation is such a recent social invention, it is not surprising that research on the subject is relatively scant. Nevertheless, some investigations comparing the outcomes of mediation and litigation have been completed, which allow some initial, albeit tentative, conclusions to be drawn (see Emery & Wyer, 1987a). The findings to date include: (1) court-based mediation programs, which focus almost exclusively on child-rearing issues, lead to a significant reduction in custody hearings—50 to 75% of parents are diverted from court by successful mediation; (2) the content of agreements reached in mediation and in litigation do not differ greatly, except that joint legal custody is a more frequent outcome of mediation; (3) compliance with agreements reached in mediation appears to be somewhat better than with settlements reached through adversarial procedures; and (4) parents, especially fathers, are generally more satisfied with their experiences with mediation than with adversarial procedures.

This last point is illustrated in the data presented in Tables 7.1, 7.2, and 7.3. These data come from a study in which parents were assigned, at random, to attempt to settle their custody and/or visitation disputes either in mediation or through adversarial procedures (Emery & Wyer, 1987b). Structured interviews containing the items listed in these tables were completed within several weeks following settlement of disputes by whatever means.

As can be seen from Table 7.1, clear and consistent differences were found for fathers between groups, since men strongly preferred mediation over adversarial procedures. It is interesting to note that these preferences extended to areas where one might expect traditional legal intervention to prevail, such as reports that one's rights had been protected. In fact, for every item in the interview, the mean response of fathers who opted for mediation indicated greater satisfaction than for fathers who, at random, were allowed to proceed through the adversary system. Furthermore, many of the differences were statistically significant and substantial in magnitude.

The data in Table 7.2 indicate that between-group differences were not as great for mothers. Mothers who went through mediation reported that the process had a significantly better effect on their children, but mothers who went through litigation felt that they had won more and lost less. This difference is partially explained by the fact that mediation is oriented toward compromise, while adversarial procedures focus on winning and losing. Nevertheless, differences

TABLE 7.1
Fathers' Reported Satisfaction with Mediation and Litigation

| | Mediation (N=17) | | Litigation (N=17) | | |
	M	SD	M	SD	F
Court process (1,27)					2.00
Satisfied with court's role	3.6	(1.3)	2.4	(1.5)	6.48**
Satisfied with own role	3.7	(1.3)	3.5	(1.3)	<1
Satisfied fairness of decisions	4.0	(.9)	3.1	(1.3)	6.19**
Feel had control over decisions	2.9	(1.5)	2.0	(1.3)	3.32*
Feel rights were protected	3.9	(1.2)	2.5	(1.2)	11.49***
Knew about available options	3.7	(1.4)	3.0	(1.5)	1.95
Court outcome (1,29)					1.01
Satisfied with decisions	3.9	(1.1)	3.1	(1.5)	
Lost what you wanted	2.2	(1.3)	2.9	(1.9)	
Won what you wanted	2.5	(1.5)	2.2	(1.8)	
Reached a lasting agreement	3.2	(1.3)	2.7	(1.8)	
Impact on self (1,29)					3.27*
Feelings were understood	3.8	(1.1)	2.5	(1.3)	9.16**
Concern was shown for you	3.4	(1.5)	2.1	(1.1)	8.15**
Court had bad effect on you	2.3	(1.5)	2.7	(1.4)	<1
Court had good effect on you	2.8	(1.6)	1.5	(1.0)	7.76**
Impact on children (1,30)					1.99
Concern was shown for kids	4.5	(1.0)	3.6	(1.3)	
Court had bad effect on kids	1.8	(1.3)	2.3	(1.3)	
Court had good effect on kids	2.6	(1.5)	1.9	(1.3)	
Impact on relationship with children's mother (1,31)					3.89*
Caused problems with spouse	1.9	(1.1)	3.2	(1.7)	7.68**
Settled problems with spouse	2.9	(1.1)	2.1	(1.4)	4.24*

*p<.05; **p<.01; ***p<.001

Items were answered on a 5-point scale where: 1=not at all; 2=a little; 3=somewhat; 4=quite a bit; 5=very much.

SOURCE: R.E. Emery & M.M. Wyer (1987b). Child custody mediation and litigation: An experimental evaluation of the experience of parents, *Journal of Consulting and Clinical Psychology*, 55, 179–186.

TABLE 7.2
Mothers' Reported Satisfaction with Mediation and Litigation

	Mediation (N=17)		Litigation (N=19)		
	M	SD	M	SD	F
Court process (1,29)					<1
Satisfied with court's role	3.5	(.9)	3.8	(1.0)	
Satisfied with own role	3.6	(1.2)	3.9	(1.0)	
Satisfied fairness of decisions	3.6	(1.2)	4.1	(1.0)	
Feel had control over decisions	3.4	(1.0)	2.9	(1.5)	
Feel rights were protected	4.1	(1.1)	4.3	(.9)	
Knew about available options	3.9	(1.3)	3.4	(1.4)	
Court outcome (1,31)					2.96*[a]
Satisfied with decisions	3.7	(.9)	4.1	(1.2)	<1
Lost what you wanted	2.7	(1.6)	1.3	(.6)	12.38***[a]
Won what you wanted	3.1	(1.4)	4.3	(1.0)	8.50**[a]
Reached a lasting agreement	2.8	(1.5)	3.3	(1.6)	<1
Impact on self (1,31)					<1
Feelings were understood	3.8	(1.1)	3.5	(1.5)	
Concern was shown for you	4.0	(1.1)	3.5	(1.3)	
Court had bad effect on you	2.3	(1.5)	2.2	(1.4)	
Court had good effect on you	3.3	(1.3)	3.0	(1.7)	
Impact on children (1,32)					2.60*
Concern was shown for kids	4.7	(.6)	4.1	(1.2)	3.05*
Court had bad effect on kids	1.2	(.6)	1.7	(.9)	2.90*
Court had good effect on kids	3.0	(1.5)	2.5	(1.6)	1.00
Impact on relationship with children's father (1,33)					<1
Caused problems with spouse	2.1	(1.4)	2.2	(1.4)	
Settled problems with spouse	3.5	(1.0)	3.5	(1.4)	

[a] This effect is the opposite from prediction.
*p<.05; **p<.01; ***p<.001

Items were answered on a 5-point scale where: 1=not at all; 2=a little; 3=somewhat; 4=quite a bit; 5=very much.

SOURCE: R.E. Emery & M.M. Wyer (1987b). Child custody mediation and litigation: An experimental evaluation of the experience of parents, *Journal of Consulting and Clinical Psychology*, **55**, 179–186.

TABLE 7.3

Comparison of Fathers' and Mothers' Evaluations of their Court Experiences

	Fathers' (N=30)[1]		Mothers'		
	M	SD	M	SD	F
Court process (1,23)					2.99*
Satisfied with court's role	3.0	(1.5)	3.7	(.9)	4.79*
Satisfied with own role	3.7	(1.2)	3.8	(1.1)	<1
Satisfied fairness of decisions	3.6	(1.1)	3.6	(1.1)	1.20
Feel had control over decisions	2.4	(1.4)	3.1	(1.3)	6.17**
Feel rights were protected	3.1	(1.4)	4.3	(.9)	17.37***
Knew about available options	3.3	(1.5)	3.7	(1.3)	1.31
Court outcome (1,25)					2.64*
Satisfied with decisions	3.5	(1.3)	4.0	(1.0)	1.90
Lost what you wanted	2.6	(1.7)	1.9	(1.3)	2.59
Won what you wanted	2.4	(1.6)	3.7	(1.3)	10.27**
Reached a lasting agreement	3.0	(1.5)	3.1	(1.5)	<1
Impact on self (1,25)					3.01*
Feelings were understood	3.1	(1.3)	3.6	(1.4)	2.27
Concern was shown for you	2.7	(1.5)	3.6	(1.2)	8.43**
Court had bad effect on you	2.5	(1.4)	2.3	(1.4)	<1
Court had good effect on you	2.1	(1.4)	3.0	(1.5)	7.75**
Impact on children (1,26)					1.47
Concern was shown for kids	4.0	(1.1)	4.4	(.9)	
Court had bad effect on kids	2.0	(1.3)	1.5	(.9)	
Court had good effect on kids	2.4	(1.5)	2.6	(1.5)	
Impact on relationship with other parent (1,27)					4.73**
Caused problems with spouse	2.6	(1.6)	2.2	(1.5)	1.90
Settled problems with spouse	2.5	(1.4)	3.5	(1.2)	9.73**

[1] Sample size is reduced since cases could only be included when data were available from both parents.

*p<.05; **p<.01; ***p<.001

Items were answered on a 5-point scale where: 1=not at all; 2=a little; 3=somewhat; 4=quite a bit; 5=very much.

SOURCE: R.E. Emery & M.M. Wyer (1987b). Child custody mediation and litigation: An experimental evaluation of the experience of parents, *Journal of Consulting and Clinical Psychology*, 55, 179–186.

between mediation and litigation were clearly not as significant for women as for men.

While calling attention to differences in mediation, these data also point to mothers' and fathers' contrasting experiences in custody hearings. As the data in Table 7.3 reveal, regardless of whether they went through mediation or adversarial procedures, women were dramatically more satisfied with the process, the outcome, and the impact of the custody determinations than were men. Comparing data from the various tables, it can be seen that fathers who went through litigation were considerably more dissatisfied than members of the other three groups. This must be due, by and large, to the fact that mothers are most likely to win custody in a court hearing. Despite our reluctance to articulate a sex preference in statutory law, the belief that mothers are preferred custodians is indicated both by case law and by normative social behavior (Emery, 1987). Mothers were awarded sole custody in 18 of the 20 litigated cases that were studied. They also negotiated sole custody in 16 of the 20 mediated cases; the remainder were joint legal custody with physical residence with the mother (Emery & Wyer, 1987b). While the actual settlements do not differ greatly from those obtained by men who litigate, the greater voice about child-rearing given to fathers in mediation brings their satisfaction into line with that experienced by mothers in either mediation or litigation (Emery & Wyer, 1987b).

The above data present an optimistic picture of divorce mediation, an alternative form of dispute settlement, but data on the effectiveness of mediation as a preventive intervention are less compelling. At least in the short run, mediation does not appear to lead to dramatic improvements in the psychological adjustment of members of divorcing families (Emery & Wyer, 1987b; Kelly, Gigy, & Hausman, in press). Nevertheless, subtle, yet important, benefits may result from mediation. The mediation process may help divorcing partners to separate their roles as parents (which are continuing) from their roles as spouses (which are coming to an end). In addition, mediation presents a good opportunity for education. Mediators serve as gatekeepers who can help to inform parents about divorce and its general and specific effects on all family members. Perhaps more importantly, mediation provides an opportunity for parents to exchange information about the children and child-rearing. In order to protect their clients' individual interests, lawyers commonly advise divorcing partners not to talk with their former spouse. While mediators also may want to limit communication in order to help the divorcing spouses to redefine interpersonal boundaries, cooperation and communication with regard to the children is encouraged.

Mediation is not a panacea, but it appears to be a step in the right direction for legal intervention in divorce. While controversies remain (Emery & Wyer, 1987a), the implementation of programs for the mediation of custody and visitation disputes should be encouraged. In fact, several states and many more local jurisdictions have made it mandatory that parents attempt to resolve their custody disputes in mediation prior to a court hearing (Emery & Wyer, 1987a). In mandatory mediation, parents remain free *not* to agree to a settlement but must make a good faith attempt to do so. In addition to diverting a significant number of families from adversarial court hearings, the idea that parents must first attempt mediation would seem to cast a new shadow over divorce disputes. The greatest ultimate influence of mandatory mediation may be that it helps to foster the expectation that divorce disputes should be settled in a cooperative manner.

UNARTICULATED NORMATIVE VALUES

Before summarizing the rather lengthy list of suggestions for policy reform discussed above, one more observation is in order. A major thesis of this chapter is that divorce law has become more general and less determinative as a result of attempts to accommodate a diversity of family values in our increasingly pluralistic society. This constitutes a retreat from "morality" in its most abstract sense, that is, the articulation and enforcement of a standard of behavior, whatever the standard might be (Schneider, 1985). Rather than specifying explicit standards to which divorcing couples are expected to conform, state legislatures have offered only very general guidelines. While such rules leave considerable latitude for individual families to order their affairs according to their own values, problems result when efforts at private ordering fail.

These points were made earlier. What has not been discussed is that, individual biases notwithstanding, there are implicit, if not explicit, norms that guide judicial determinations (and which, therefore, strongly influence settlements made out of court). Officially unarticulated preferences in favor of maternal custody have been mentioned already, and there are similar "rules of thumb" that guide judicial decisions concerning visitation frequency, child support, and property division (Weitzman, 1985). While the implicit rules vary somewhat from judge to judge, jurisdiction to jurisdiction, and state to state, what is most remarkable is the consistency of judicial practice in the absence of a clear articulation of legislative preferences.

This consistency does not suggest that the judiciary is imposing its own idiosyncratic values on the public. Rather, the reverse would seem to be true. That is, the judiciary seems to be conforming to unarticulated social norms. For example, while a preference for mothers as custodians is no longer articulated in statutory law, case law and judicial opinion continue to indicate such a preference (Emery, 1987). Moreover, the cultural assumption persists that, subsequent to divorce, mothers should raise their children. Consider the social pressures women face if they decide that they do *not* want custody. Even in Iran, where a father's legal right to the custody of his children upon divorce remains unquestioned, mothers retain custody of their children in 70% cases (Aghajanian, 1986)!

Given the fact that social behavior clearly conforms to unstated norms, why our legislatures cannot articulate standards is an intriguing question that cannot be addressed here. Suffice it to say that greater clarity in our social consensus—whatever the moral content may be—would have at least some desirable consequences. Given the probability that a strong moral code will not be forthcoming in the very near future, is there a step that can be taken which will accommodate diversity while removing uncertainty?

There may be. Perhaps the data on divorce settlements should be published, judge by judge, jurisdiction by jurisdiction, state by state. Data could be aggregated to protect the privacy of individual families, and publication of the averages might have several desirable consequences. If judges are awarding (or no longer awarding) custody to mothers, that information should be in the public domain. If yearly statistics indicated that only 15% women receive spousal support, this would decimate the "alimony myth." If young women knew they would have primary responsibility for the economic and emotional care of their children following divorce (or if young men knew that their responsibilities were going to be enforced), they might make the same choices they make now, but at least these would be informed choices.

The publication of such statistics would still leave each individual family free to construct its own divorce settlement. There should be no attempt to coerce anyone to follow the norm. Still, whether they settle inside or outside of court, if normative information were available, family members would at least know where they stood relative to others. The public would also know where individual judges stood with regard to judicial norms, and this should discourage the abuse of discretion. How divorcing families *should* behave would remain unarticulated, but how divorcing families—and the professionals who help them to order their affairs—*do* behave, would become explicit rather than implicit. This may produce beneficial consequences at a minimal cost.

SUMMARY OF SUGGESTIONS FOR LEGAL POLICIES

Legal policies with respect to the regulation of divorce, standards for settling financial and child-rearing disputes, and the process by which disputes are settled were examined in this chapter. Several concerns have been raised about current policy, and general directions for changes suggested. The following are among the suggestions for policy initiatives:

With reference to the regulation of divorce, rolling back no-fault divorce laws is an unlikely and undesirable alternative. Numerous naturalistic disincentives to divorce already exist, ranging from economic consequences to parental concerns about their children. Rather than adding artificial disincentives, a more fruitful approach would be the provision of incentives to remain married. Since the major concern is the care of children, it seems best to develop policies which focus on the fulfillment of parental responsibilities inside or outside marriage. Policies which, for example, mandate that biological parents must provide financial support for their children would not only help to alter the consequences of divorce, but would also begin to address the economic problems of children born out of wedlock. It is worth noting that strict requirements for fulfilling parental responsibilities, and stringent enforcement of these requirements, would also serve as disincentives for nonresidential parents to divorce.

As for financial settlements, the expanded definitions of marital property and the equal division of assets ought to lead to settlements that are fairer in the individual case, but changes in the way that marital property is divided and spousal support paid are unlikely to have a dramatic effect on the postdivorce economic situation of children. While clearer definitions of what constitutes marital property and what rules should govern its division would be helpful, perhaps the major legislative contribution here would be to state a preference against selling the family home to facilitate property division, subject to certain exceptions.

While child support is not likely to change children's living standards dramatically, it certainly can improve them. Some strong enforcement policies are already being implemented. What is needed, in addition, is a clear formula for determining support amounts and automatic collection systems. A "child tax" for nonresidential parents may be the best avenue to pursue. Finally, a major improvement in children's postdivorce living standards could come from the general enhancement of women's employment. Nevertheless, sex disparities, the limited support available to single-parent families, and economies of scale do and will continue to provide economic incentives for remarriage. While remarriage ought not to be the only economic solution, it would be foolish to ignore its importance.

With reference to child-rearing disputes, several changes have been suggested in this book, given the absence of a clear standard for determining sole custody. First, there should be a presumption in favor of joint legal custody upon separation/divorce, unless custody is contested before a judge. At this point, the presumption would switch to sole custody plus visitation. Because custody disputes per se can be harmful to children, and because the real concern for child-rearing is the quality not the quantity of parenting, policies which mandate that parents first attempt to resolve their disputes in mediation should also be encouraged. Combined with the presumption of joint legal custody, mandatory mediation laws should help to change attitudes about postdivorce parenting. As for physical custody, education about options is perhaps the major policy tool available.

Finally, even though formal standards have not been articulated to date, settlements nevertheless seem to conform to unarticulated norms. It is therefore suggested that aggregate statistics on contested and uncontested divorce settlements be published judge by judge, jurisdiction by jurisdiction, and state by state. This would help to limit abuse in the exercise of judicial discretion, more fully inform divorcing partners about likely settlement options, and, most importantly, educate youth about the implicit terms of the marriage contract.

At the very beginning of this book it was suggested that interventions in divorce should be based on what is known, not on what is assumed. The final recommendation for policy, therefore, is to continue the investigation of marriage, divorce, and children at several levels of understanding.

REFERENCES

Achenbach, T. M., McConaughy, S.H., & Howell, C. T. (1987). Child/adolescent behavioral and emotional problems: Implications of cross-informant correlations for situational specificity. *Psychological Bulletin, 101*, 213–232.

Aghajanian, A. (1986). Some notes on divorce in Iran. *Journal of Marriage and the Family, 48*, 749–756.

Ainsworth, M.D.S. (1979). Infant-mother attachment. *American Psychologist, 34*, 932–937.

Ambert, A. (1984). Longitudinal changes in children's behavior toward custodial parents. *Journal of Marriage and the Family, 46*, 463–467.

Anderson, S. A., Russell, C. S., & Schumm, W. R. (1983). Perceived marital quality and family life-cycle categories: A further analysis. *Journal of Marriage and the Family, 45*, 127–139.

Aries, P. (1962). *Centuries of Childhood: A social history of family life*. Translated by Robert Baldick. New York: Knopf.

Baltes, P. B., Cornelius, S. W., & Nesselroade, J. R. (1979). Cohort effects in developmental psychology. In J. R. Nesselroade, & P. B. Baltes (Eds.), *Longitudinal research in the study of behavior and development* (pp. 61–88). New York: Academic.

Bane, M. J. (1979). Marital disruption and the lives of children. In G. Levinger, & O. C. Moles (Eds.), *Divorce and separation* (pp. 276–286). New York: Basic.

Befera, M. S., & Barkley, R. A. (1985). Hyperactive and normal girls and boys: Mother-child interaction, parent psychiatric status, and child psychopathology. *Journal of Child Psychology and Psychiatry, 26*, 439–452.

Belsky, J., & Isabella, R. A. (1985). Marital and parent-child relationships in family of origin and marital change following the birth of a baby: A retrospective analysis. *Child Development, 56*, 342–349.

Berg, B., & Kelly, R. (1979). Measured self-esteem of children from broken, rejected, and accepted families. *Journal of Divorce, 2*, 363–370.

Bilge, B., & Kaufman, G. (1983). Children of divorce and one-parent families: Cross-cultural perspectives. *Family Relations, 32*, 59–71.

Biller, H. B. (1969). Father absence, maternal encouragement, and sex-role development in kindergarten boys. *Child Development, 40*, 539–546.

Biller, H. B., & Bahm, R. M. (1971). Father absence, perceived maternal behavior, and masculinity of self-concept among junior high school boys. *Developmental Psychology, 4*, 178–181.

Blechman, E. A. (1982). Are children with one parent at psychological risk? A methodological review. *Journal of Marriage and the Family, 44*, 179–195.

Block, J. H., Block, J., & Gjerde, P. F. (1986). The personality of children prior to divorce: A prospective study. *Child Development, 57,* 827–840.

Block, J. H., Block, J., & Morrison, A. (1981). Parental agreement-disagreement on child-rearing orientations and gender-related personality correlates in children. *Child Development, 52,* 965–974.

Bloom, B. L., Asher, S. J., & White, S. W. (1978). Marital disruption as a stressor: A review and analysis. *Psychological Bulletin, 85,* 867–894.

Bloom, B. L., Hodges, W. F., & Caldwell, R. A. (1982). A preventive intervention program for the newly separated: Initial evaluation. *American Journal of Community Psychology, 10,* 251–264.

Bloom, B. L., Hodges, W. F., Kern, M. B., & McFaddin, S. C. (1985). A preventive intervention program for the newly separated: Final evaluation. *American Journal of Orthopsychiatry, 55,* 9–26.

Booth, A., Binkerhoff, D. B., & White, L. K. (1984). The impact of parental divorce on courtship. *Journal of Marriage and the Family, 46,* 85–94.

Bowlby, J. (1951). *Maternal care and mental health.* Geneva: WHO.

Bowlby, J. (1973). *Attachment and loss (vol. 2): Separation.* New York: Basic.

Bowlby, J. (1979). *The making and breaking of affectional bonds.* London: Tavistock.

Bowlby, J. (1980). *Attachment and loss (vol. 3): Loss, Sadness, and Depression.* New York: Basic.

Bowman, M. E., & Ahrons, C. R. (1985). Impact of legal custody status on fathers' parenting postdivorce. *Journal of Marriage and the Family, 47,* 481–488.

Braver, S., Gonzalez, N., Sandler, I., & Wolchik, S. (1985, February). Economic hardship and postdivorce adjustment of custodial mothers. Paper presented to the Third Annual Conference on Family Competence, Arizona State University.

Brody, G. H., & Forehand, R. (1985). The efficacy of parent training with maritally distressed and nondistressed mothers: A multimethod assessment. *Behaviour Research and Therapy, 23,* 291–296.

Bumpass, L. (1984a). Children and marital disruption: A replication and update. *Demography, 21,* 71–82.

Bumpass, L. (1984b). Some characteristics of children's second families. *American Journal of Sociology, 90,* 608–623.

Bumpass, L., & Rindfuss, R. R. (1979). Children's experience of marital disruption. *American Journal of Sociology, 85,* 49–65.

Burger, W. B. (1982). Isn't there a better way? *American Bar Association Journal, 68,* 274–277.

Burgess, R. L. (1978). *Project interact: A study of patterns of interaction in abusive, neglectful, and control families* (Final Report). Washington, D.C.: National Center on Child Abuse and Neglect.

Camara, K. A. (1985, April). Social knowledge and behavior of children in single-parent and two-parent households. Paper presented at 62nd Annual Meeting of the American Orthopsychiatric Association. New York.

Camara, K. A., & Resnick, G. (in press, a). Interparental conflict and cooperation: Factors moderating children's postdivorce adjustment. In E. M. Hetherington, & J. Arasteh (Eds.), *Divorced, single-parent, and stepparent families.* Hillsdale, NJ: Lawrence Erlbaum.

Camara, K. A., & Resnick, G. (in press, b). Marital and parental subsystems in mother-custody, father-custody, and two-parent households: Effects on children's social development. In J. Vincent (Ed.), *Advances in family assessment, intervention and research* (vol. 4). Greenwich, CT: JAI.

Carlsmith, L. (1964). Effect of early father absence on scholastic achievement. *Harvard Educational Review, 34,* 3–21.

Chambers, D. (1979). *Making fathers pay: The enforcement of child support.* Chicago: University of Chicago Press.

Chang, P., & Deinard, A. S. (1982). Single-father caretakers: Demographic characteristics and adjustment processes. *American Journal of Orthopsychiatry, 52,* 236–243.

Chapman, M. (1977). Father absence, stepfathers, and the cognitive performance of college students. *Child Development, 48,* 1155–1158.

Cherlin, A. J. (1977). The effect of children on marital dissolution. *Demography, 14,* 265–272.

Cherlin, A. J. (1981). *Marriage, divorce, remarriage.* Cambridge, MA: Harvard University Press.

Chess, S., Thomas, A., Korn, S., Mittelman, M., & Cohen, H. (1983). Early parental attitudes, divorce and separation, and young adult outcome: Findings of a longitudinal study. *Journal of the American Academy of Child Psychiatry, 22,* 47–51.

Christopoulos, C., Cohn, D. A., Shaw, D. S., Joyce, S., Kraft, S. P., & Emery, R. E. (1987). Children of battered women I: Adjustment at time of shelter residence. *Journal of Marriage and the Family, 49,* 611–619.

Clingempeel, W. G., Brand, E., & Ievoli, R. (1984). Stepparent-stepchild relationships in stepmother and stepfather families: A multimethod study. *Family Relations, 33,* 465–473.

Clingempeel, W. G., & Reppucci, N. D. (1982). Joint custody after divorce: Major issues and goals for research. *Psychological Bulletin, 91,* 102–127.

Colletta, N. D. (1979). The impact of divorce: Father absence or poverty? *Journal of Divorce, 3,* 27–35.

Cooper, J. E., Holman, J., & Braithwaite, V. A. (1983). Self-esteem and family cohesion: The child's perspective and adjustment. *Journal of Marriage and the Family, 45,* 153–159.

Crook, T., & Eliot, J. (1980). Parental death during childhood and adult depression: A critical review of the literature. *Psychological Bulletin, 87,* 252–259.

Cummings, E. M., Iannotti, R. J., & Zahn-Waxler, C. (1985). The influence of conflict between adults on the emotions and aggression of young children. *Developmental Psychology, 21,* 495–507.

Cummings, E. M., Zahn-Waxler, C., & Radke-Yarrow, M. (1981). Young children's responses to expressions of anger and affection by others in the family. *Child Development, 52,* 1274–1282.

Cummings, E. M., Zahn-Waxler, C., & Radke-Yarrow, M. (1984). Developmental changes in children's reactions to anger in the home. *Journal of Child Psychology and Psychiatry, 25,* 63–74.

Dadds, M. R., Schwartz, S., & Sanders, M. R. (1987). Marital discord and treatment outcome in behavioral treatment of child conduct disorders. *Journal of Consulting and Clinical Psychology, 55,* 396–403.

Derdeyn, A. P. (1976). Child custody contests in historical perspective. *American Journal of Psychiatry, 133,* 1369–1376.

Desimone-Luis, J., O'Mahoney, K., & Hunt, D. (1979). Children of separation and divorce: Factors influencing adjustment. *Journal of Divorce, 3,* 37–42.

Douglas, J.W.B., Ross, T. M., Hammond, W. A., & Mulligan, D. G. (1966). Delinquency and social class. *British Journal of Criminology, 6*, 294–302.

Duncan, G. J., & Hoffman, S. D. (1985). Economic consequences of marital instability. In M. David & T. Smeeding (Eds.), *Horizontal equity, uncertainty and well-being* (pp. 427–469). Chicago: University of Chicago Press.

Duncan, G. J. & Morgan, J. N. (1976a). Introduction and overview. In G. J. Duncan & J. N. Morgan (Eds.), *Five thousand American families—Patterns of economic progress* (vol. 4, pp. 1–22). Ann Arbor: Institute for Social Research.

Duncan, G. J., & Morgan, J. N. (1976b). Young children and "other" family members. In G. J. Duncan & J. N. Morgan (Eds.), *Five thousand American families—Patterns of economic progress* (vol. 4, pp. 155–179). Ann Arbor: Institute for Social Research.

Elder, G. H., Caspi, A., & Downey, G. (1984). Problem behavior and family relationships: A multigenerational analysis. In A. Sorensen, F. Weinert, & L. Sherrod (Eds.), *Human development: Interdisciplinary perspectives*. New York: Springer.

Ellwood, D. T., & Bane, M. J. (1985). The impact of AFDC on family structure and living arrangements. Unpublished manuscript, Harvard University.

Emery, R. E. (1982). Interparental conflict and the children of discord and divorce. *Psychological Bulletin, 92*, 310–330.

Emery, R. E. (1987, April). The legal system's conception of childhood in custody disputes. Paper presented at the annual meeting of the Society for Research in Child Development, Baltimore.

Emery, R. E., Binkoff, J. A., Houts, A. C., & Carr, E. G. (1983). Children as independent variables: Some clinical implications of child effects. *Behavior Therapy, 14*, 398–412.

Emery, R. E., Hetherington, E. M., & DiLalla, L. F. (1984). Divorce, children, and social policy. In H. W. Stevenson & A. E. Siegel (Eds.), *Child development research and social policy* (pp. 189–266). Chicago: University of Chicago Press.

Emery, R. E., Joyce, S. A., & Fincham, F. D. (1987). The assessment of marital and child problems. In K. D. O'Leary (Ed.), *Assessment of marital discord* (pp. 223–262). Hillsdale, N. J.: Lawrence Erlbaum.

Emery, R. E. & O'Leary, K. D. (1984). Marital discord and child behavior problems in a nonclinic sample. *Journal of Abnormal Child Psychology, 12*, 411–420.

Emery, R. E., Shaw, D. S., & Jackson, J. A. (in press). A clinical description of a model for the co-mediation of child-custody disputes. In J. Vincent (Ed.), *Advances in family intervention, assessment, and theory* (vol. 4). Greenwich, CT: JAI.

Emery, R. E., Weintraub, S., & Neale, J. M. (1982). Effects of marital discord on the school behavior of children of schizophrenic, affectively disordered, and normal parents. *Journal of Abnormal Child Psychology, 10*, 215–228.

Emery, R. E., & Wyer, M. M. (1987a). Divorce mediation. *American Psychologist, 42*, 472–480.

Emery, R. E., & Wyer, M. M. (1987b). Child-custody mediation and litigation: An experimental evaluation of the experience of parents. *Journal of Consulting and Clinical Psychology, 55*, 179–186.

Empey, L. T. (1976). The social construction of childhood, delinquency and social reform. In M. Klein (Ed.), *The juvenile justice system*. Beverly Hills: Sage.

Engels, F. (1942, 1970). *The origin of the family, private property, and the state.* New York: International Publishers Company.

Enos, D. M. & Handal, P. J. (1986). The relation of parental marital status and perceived family conflict to adjustment in white adolescents. *Journal of Consulting and Clinical Psychology, 54,* 820–824.

Espenshade, T. J. (1979). The economic consequences of divorce. *Journal of Marriage and the Family, 41,* 615–625.

Farrington, D. P. (1979). Longitudinal research on crime and delinquency. In N. Morris & M. Tonry (Eds.), *Criminal justice: An annual review of research* (vol. 1, pp. 289–348). Chicago: University of Chicago Press.

Featherman, D. L. & Hauser, R. M. (1978). *Opportunity and change.* New York: Academic.

Feldman, S. S., Biringen, Z. C., & Nash, S. C. (1981). Fluctuations of sex-related self-attributions, a function of stage of family life cycle. *Developmental Psychology, 17,* 24–35.

Felner, R. D., Farber, S. S., & Primavera, J. (1980). Children of divorce, stressful life events and transitions: A framework for preventive efforts. In R. H. Price, R. F. Ketterer, B. C. Bader, & J. Monahan (Eds.), *Prevention in mental health: Research, policy, and practice* (vol. 1, pp. 81–108). Beverly Hills, CA: Sage.

Felner, R. D., Stolberg, A., & Cowen, E. L. (1975). Crisis events and school mental health referral patterns of young children. *Journal of Consulting and Clinical Psychology, 43,* 305–310.

Fergusson, D. M., Dimond, M. E., & Horwood, L. J. (1986). Childhood family placement history and behavior problems in 6-year-old children. *Journal of Child Psychology and Psychiatry, 27,* 213–226.

Ferri, E. (1976). *Growing up in a one-parent family: A long-term study of child development.* London: National Foundation for Educational Research.

Folberg, J. (1984). *Joint custody and shared parenting.* Washington, D.C.: BNA.

Foster, H. H., & Freed, D. J. (1973–74). Divorce reform: Breaks on breakdown. *Journal of Family Law, 74,* 443–493.

Freed, D. J., & Foster, H. H. (1981). Divorce in the fifty states: An overview. *Family Law Quarterly, 14,* 229–241.

Freed, D. J., & Foster, H. H. (1984). Family law in the fifty states: An overview. *Family Law Quarterly, 17,* 365–447.

Freed, D. J., & Walker, T. B. (1986). Family law in the fifty states: An overview. *Family Law Quarterly, 19,* 331–411.

Furstenberg, F. F. (1985). Sociological ventures in child development. *Child Development, 56,* 281–288.

Furstenberg, F. F. (1987). The new extended family: The experience of parents and children after remarriage. In K. Palsey & M. Ihinger-Tallman (Eds.), *Remarriage and Stepparenting today: Current research and theory* (pp. 42–61). New York: Guilford.

Furstenberg, F. F., & Allison, P. D. (1985). How marital dissolution affects children: Variations by age and sex. Unpublished manuscript, University of Pennsylvania.

Furstenberg, F. F., Morgan, S. P., & Allison, P. D. (1987, April). Paternal participation and children's well-being after marital disruption. Paper presented at the annual meeting of the Population Association of America, Chicago.

Furstenberg, F. F., & Nord, C. W. (1985). Parenting apart: Patterns of child-rearing after marital disruption. *Journal of Marriage and the Family, 47,* 893–904.

Furstenberg, F. F., Peterson, J. L., Nord, C. W., & Zill, N., (1983). The life course of children of divorce: Marital disruption and parental contact. *American Sociological Review, 48*, 656–668.

Furstenberg, F. F., & Spanier, G. B. (1984). *Recycling the family: Remarriage after divorce*. Beverly Hills: Sage.

Ganong, L. H., & Coleman, M. (1984). The effects of remarriage on children: A review of the empirical literature. *Family Relations, 33*, 389–406.

Gersick, K. E. (1979). Fathers by choice: Divorced men who receive custody of their children. In G. Levinger & O. C. Moles (Eds.), *Divorce and separation* (pp. 307–323). New York: Basic Books.

Gibson, H. B. (1969). Early delinquency in relation to broken homes. *Journal of Child Psychology and Psychiatry, 10*, 195–204.

Gjerde, P. F. (1986). The interpersonal structure of family interaction settings: Parent-adolescent relations in dyads and triads. *Developmental Psychology, 22*, 297–304.

Glendon, M. A. (1980). Modern marriage law and its underlying assumptions: The new marriage and the new property. *Family Law Quarterly, 13*, 441–460.

Glenn, N. D., & Kramer, K. B. (1985). The psychological well-being of adult children of divorce. *Journal of Marriage and the Family, 47*, 905–912.

Glenn, N. D., & McLanahan (1981). The effects of offspring on the psychological well-being of older adults. *Journal of Marriage and the Family, 43*, 409–421.

Glenn, N. D., & McLanahan (1982). Children and marital happiness: A further specification of the relationship. *Journal of Marriage and the Family, 44*, 63–72.

Glick, P. C. (1979). Children of divorced parents in demographic perspective. *Journal of Social Issues, 35*, 112–125.

Glick, P. C. (1984). How American families are changing. *American Demographics, 6*, 20–27.

Glick, P. C., & Lin, S. (1986). Recent changes in divorce and remarriage. *Journal of Marriage and the Family, 48*, 737–747.

Glueck, S., & Glueck, E. (1950). *Unraveling juvenile delinquency*. Cambridge, MA: Harvard University Press.

Goldstein, H. S. (1984). Parental composition, supervision, and conduct problems in youths 12 to 17 years old. *Journal of the American Academy of Child Psychiatry, 23*, 679–684.

Goldstein, J., Freud, A., & Solnit, A. J. (1973). *Beyond the best interests of the child*. New York: Free Press.

Goode, W. J. (1968). Industrialization and family structure. In N. W. Bell & E. F. Vogel (Eds.), *A modern introduction to the family*. New York: Free Press.

Greenberg, E. F., & Nay, W. R. (1982). The intergenerational transmission of marital instability reconsidered. *Journal of Marriage and the Family, 44*, 335–347.

Gregory, I. (1965). Anterospective data following childhood loss of a parent: Delinquency and high school dropout. *Archives of General Psychiatry, 13*, 99–109.

Greif, J. B. (1979). Fathers, children, and joint custody. *American Journal of Orthopsychiatry, 49*, 311–319.

Griest, D. L., Forehand, R., Rogers, T., Breiner, J., Furey, W., & Williams, C. A. (1982). Effects of parent enhancement therapy on the treatment outcome and generalization of a parent training program. *Behaviour Research and Therapy, 20*, 429–436.

Guidubaldi, J., Perry, J. D., & Cleminshaw, H. K. (1984). The legacy of parental divorce: A nationwide study of family status and selected mediating variables on children's academic and social competencies. In B. B. Lahey & A. E. Kazdin (Eds.), *Advances in child clinical psychology* (vol. 7, pp. 109–155). New York: Plenum.

Gurman, A. S., Kniskern, D. P., & Pinsof, W. M. (1986). Research on marital and family therapies. In S. L. Garfield & A. E. Bergin (Eds.), *Handbook of psychotherapy and behavior change* (pp. 565–626). New York: Wiley.

Hainline, L., & Feig, E. (1978). The correlates of childhood father absence in college-aged women. *Child Development, 49,* 37–42.

Halem, L. C. (1981). *Divorce reform.* New York: Free Press.

Hannan, M. T., Tuma, N. B., & Groeneveld, L. P. (1977). Income and marital events: Evidence from the income-maintenance experiment. *American Journal of Sociology, 82,* 1186–1211.

Hareven, T. (1986). Historical changes in the family and the life course: Implications for child development. *Monographs of the Society for Research in Child Development, 50,* 8–23.

Harris, T., Brown, G. W., & Bifulco, A. (1986). Loss of parent in childhood and adult psychiatric disorder: The role of lack of adequate parental care. *Psychological Medicine, 16,* 641–659.

Herzog, E., & Sudia, C. E. (1973). Children in fatherless families. In B. Caldwell & H. Ricciuti (Eds.), *Review of child development research* (vol. 3, pp. 141–232). Chicago: University of Chicago Press.

Hess, R. D., & Camara, K. A. (1979). Postdivorce relationships as mediating factors in the consequences of divorce for children. *Journal of Social Issues, 35,* 79–96.

Hetherington, E. M. (1972). Effects of parental absence on personality development in adolescent daughters. *Developmental Psychology, 7,* 313–326.

Hetherington, E. M. (1979). Divorce: A child's perspective. *American Psychologist, 34,* 851–858.

Hetherington, E. M. (1986). Family relations six years after divorce. In K. Pasley & M. Ihinger-Tallman (Eds.), *Remarriage and stepparenting today: Research and theory* (pp. 185–205). New York: Guilford.

Hetherington, E. M., Camara, K. A., & Featherman, D. L. (1981). Achievement and intellectual functioning of children in one-parent households. In J. Spence (Ed.), *Assessing achievement.* New York: Freeman.

Hetherington, E. M., Cox, M., & Cox, R. (1976). Divorced fathers. *Family Coordinator, 25,* 417–428.

Hetherington, E. M., Cox, M., & Cox, R. (1978). The aftermath of divorce. In J. H. Stevens & M. Matthews (Eds.), *Mother-child, father-child relations* (pp. 110–155). Washington, D.C.: National Association for the Education of Young Children.

Hetherington, E. M., Cox, M., & Cox, R. (1979). Family interaction and the social, emotional, and cognitive development of children following divorce. In V. Vaughn & T. Brazelton (Eds.), *The family: Setting priorities* (pp. 89–128). New York: Science and Medicine.

Hetherington, E. M., Cox, M., & Cox, R. (1982). Effects of divorce on parents and children. In M. Lamb (Ed.), *Nontraditional families* (pp. 233–288). Hillsdale, NJ: Lawrence Erlbaum.

Hetherington, E. M., Cox, M., & Cox, R. (1985). Long-term effects of divorce and remarriage on the adjustment of children. *Journal of the American Academy of Child Psychiatry, 24,* 518–530.

Hodges, W. F. (1986). *Interventions for children of divorce.* New York: Wiley.

Hodges, W. F., Wechsler, R. C., & Ballantine, C. (1979). Divorce and the preschool child: Cumulative stress. *Journal of Divorce, 3,* 55–67.

Hoffman, M. L. (1971). Father absence and conscience development. *Developmental Psychology, 4,* 400–406.

Hoffman. S. (1977). Marital instability and the economic status of women. *Demography, 14,* 67–76.

Huston, A. C. (1983). Sex typing. In E. M. Hetherington (Ed.), *Handbook of child psychology* (4th. Ed., pp. 387–467). New York: Wiley.

Ilfeld, F. W., Ilfeld, H. Z., & Alexander, J. R. (1982). Does joint custody work? A first look at outcome data of relitigation. *American Journal of Psychiatry, 139,* 62–66.

Irving, H. H., Benjamin, M., & Trocme, N. (1984). Shared parenting: An empirical analysis utilizing a large data base. *Family Process, 23,* 561–569.

Jacobs, J. A., & Furstenberg, F. F. (1986). Changing places: Conjugal careers and women's marital mobility. *Social Forces, 64,* 714–732.

Jacobs, J. W. (1986). Divorce and child custody resolution: Conflicting legal and psychological paradigms. *American Journal of Psychiatry, 143,* 192–197.

Jacobson, D. S. (1978). The impact of marital separation/divorce on children. II: Interparental hostility and child adjustment. *Journal of Divorce, 2,* 3–19.

Jencks. C. (1972). *Inequality: A reassessment of the effect of family and schooling in America.* New York: Harper.

Johnston, J. R., Campbell, E. G., & Mayes, S. S. (1985). Latency children in postseparation and divorce disputes. *Journal of the American Academy of Child Psychiatry, 24,* 563–574.

Kagan, J. (1984). *The nature of the child.* New York: Basic Books.

Kalmuss, D. (1984). The intergenerational transmission of marital aggression. *Journal of Marriage and the Family, 47,* 11–19.

Kalter, N. (1977). Children of divorce in an outpatient psychiatric population. *American Journal of Orthopsychiatry, 47,* 50–51.

Kalter, N., & Rembar, J. (1981). The significance of a child's age at the time of parental divorce. *American Journal of Orthopsychiatry, 51,* 85–100.

Kalter, N., Riemer, B., Brickman, A., & Chen, J. W. (1985). Implications of parental divorce for female development. *Journal of the American Academy of Child Psychiatry, 24,* 538–544.

Kelly, J. B., & Wallerstein, J. S. (1976). The effects of parental divorce I: The experience of the child in early latency. *American Journal of Orthopsychiatry, 45,* 253–265.

Kelly, J. B., Gigy, L., & Hausman, S. (in press). Mediated and adversarial divorce. Initial findings from the divorce and mediation project. In J. Folberg & A. Milne (Eds.), *Divorce mediation: Theory and practice.* New York: Guilford.

Kessen, W. (1979). The American child and other cultural innovations. *American Psychologist, 34,* 815–820.

Kitson, G. C., & Langlie, J. D. (1984). Couples who file for divorce but change their minds. *American Journal of Orthopsychiatry, 54,* 469–489.

Kressel, K. (1985). *The process of divorce: How professionals and couples negotiate settlement.* New York: Basic Books.

Kurdek, L. A. (in press). Custodial mothers' perceptions of visitation and payment of child support by noncustodial fathers in families with low and high levels of preseparation interparent conflict. *Journal of Applied Developmental Psychology.*

Kurdek, L. A., & Berg, B. (in press). The Children's Beliefs about Parental Divorce Scale: Psychometric characteristics and concurrent validity. *Journal of Consulting and Clinical Psychology.*

Kurdek, L. A., Blisk, D., & Siesky, A. E. (1981). Correlates of children's long-term adjustment to their parents' divorce. *Developmental Psychology, 17,* 565–579.

Kulka, R. A., & Weingarten, H. (1979). The long-term effects of parental divorce in childhood on adult adjustment. *Journal of Social Issues, 35,* 50–78.

Lamb, M. E. (1977). The effects of divorce on children's personality development. *Journal of Divorce, 1,* 163–174.

Lambert, L., Essen, J., & Head, J. (1977). Variations in behavior ratings of children who have been in care. *Journal of Child Psychology and Psychiatry, 18,* 335–346.

Lambert, L., & Hart, S. (1976). Who needs a father? *New Society, 37,* 80.

Landsman, K. J., & Minow, M. L. (1978). Lawyering for the child: Principles of representation in custody and visitation disputes arising from divorce, *Yale Law Journal, 87,* 1126–1190.

Levitin. T. E. (1979). Children of divorce. *Journal of Social Issues, 35,* 1–25.

Long, N., Forehand, R., Fauber, R., & Brody, G. H. (in press). Self-perceived and independently observed competence of young adolescents as a function of parental marital conflict and recent divorce. *Journal of Abnormal Child Psychology.*

Luepnitz, D. A. (1982). *Child custody: A study of families after divorce.* Lexington, MA: Lexington Books.

Maccoby, E. E., & Martin, J. A. (1983). Socialization in the context of the family: Parent-child interaction. In E. M. Hetherington (Ed.), *Handbook of child psychology* (4th. Ed., vol. 4, pp. 1–102.). New York: Wiley.

Maccoby, E. E., & Mnookin, R. (1986, May). Custody settlements in a California sample. Paper presented at the annual meeting of the American Association for Advancement of Science, Philadelphia.

Maccoby, E. E., & Rau, L. (1962). *Differential cognitive abilities.* (Cooperative Research Project No. 1040). Washington: Office of Education.

MacKinnon, C. E., Brody, G. H., & Stoneman, Z. (1982). The effects of divorce and maternal employment on the home environments of preschool children. *Child Development, 53,* 1392–1399.

Margolin, G., & Christensen, A. (1981, November). The treatment of families with marital and child problems. Paper presented at the annual meeting of the Association for the Advancement of Behavior Therapy. Toronto.

McArdle, J. J., & Epstein, D. (1987). Latent growth curves within developmental structural equation models. *Child Development, 58,* 110–133.

McCord, J., McCord, W., & Thurber, E. (1962). Some effects of paternal absence on male children. *Journal of Abnormal and Social Psychology, 64,* 361–369.

McDermott, J. F. (1968). Parental divorce in early childhood. *American Journal of Psychiatry, 124,* 1424–1432.

McDermott, J. F. (1970). Divorce and its psychiatric sequence in children. *Archives of General Psychiatry, 23,* 421–427.

McHenry, P. C., Herrman, M. S., & Weber, R. E. (1978). Attitudes of attorneys toward divorce issues. *Conciliation Courts Review, 16*, 11–17.

Meehl, P. E., & Rosen, A. (1955). Antecedent probability and the efficiency of psychmetric signs, patterns, or cutting scores. *Psychological Bulletin, 52*, 194–216.

Meissner, W. W. (1978). Conceptualization of marriage and family dynamics from a psychoanalytic perspective. In T. J. Paolino & B. S. McCrady (Eds.), *Marriage and marital therapy* (pp. 25–88). New York: Brunner/Mazel.

Miller, W. B. (1958). Lower class culture as a generating milieu of gang delinquency. *Journal of Social Issues, 14*, 5–19.

Minuchin, P. (1985). Families and individual development: Provocations from the field of family therapy. *Child Development, 56*, 289–302.

Minuchin, S., Baker, L., Rosman, B. L., Liebman, R., Milman, L., & Todd, T. G. (1975). A conceptual model of psychosomatic illness in children: Family organization and family therapy. *Archives of General Psychiatry, 32*, 1031–1038.

Mnookin, R. H. (1975). Child-custody adjudication: Judicial functions in the face of indeterminancy. *Law and Contemporary Problems, 88*, 226–293.

Mnookin, R. H., & Kornhauser, L. (1979). Bargaining in the shadow of the law: The case of divorce. *Yale Law Journal, 88*, 950–997.

Mueller, C., & Pope, H. (1977). Marital instability: A study of its transmission between generations. *Journal of Marriage and the Family, 39*, 83–93.

National Center for Health Statistics (1972). *Behavior patterns of children in school.* (Vital and Health Statistics, PHS Publication Series 11. no. 113). Washington: U.S. Government Printing Office.

National Institute for Child Support Enforcement (NICSE) (1986). *History and fundamentals of child-support enforcement* (2nd. Ed.). Washington: U.S. Government Printing Office.

Newcomer, S., & Udry, J. R. (1987). Parental marital status effects on adolescent sexual behavior. *Journal of Marriage and the Family, 49*, 235–240.

Nicholas-Casebolt, A. (1986). The economic impact of child-support reform on the poverty status of custodial and noncustodial families. *Journal of Marriage and the Family, 48*, 875–880.

Norton, A. J., & Glick, P. C. (1979). Marital instability in America: Past, present and future. In G. Levinger & O. C. Moles, (Eds.), *Divorce and separation* (pp. 6–19). New York: Basic.

Nye, F. I. (1957). Child adjustment in broken and in unhappy unbroken homes. *Marriage and Family Living, 19*, 356–360.

O'Connell, M., & Rogers, C. C. (1984). Out-of-wedlock births, premarital pregnancies, and their effect on family formation and dissolution. *Family Planning Perspectives, 16*, 157–162.

Ogburn, W. F. (1953). *The changing functions of the family: Selected studies in marriage and the family.* New York: Holt.

O'Leary, K. D., & Emery, R. E. (1984). Marital discord and child behavior problems. In M. D. Levine & P. Satz (Eds.), *Middle childhood: Development and dysfunction* (pp. 345–364). Baltimore: University Park Press.

Oltmanns, T. F., Broderick, J. E., & O'Leary, K. D. (1977). Marital adjustment and the efficacy of behavior therapy with children. *Journal of Consulting and Clinical Psychology, 45*, 724–729.

Orthner, D., Brown, R., & Ferguson, D. (1976). Single-parent fatherhood: An emerging family life style. *Family Coordinator, 25*, 429–437.

Oshman, H. P., & Manosevitz, M. (1976). Father absence: Effects of stepfathers upon psychosocial development in males. *Development Psychology, 12*, 479–480.

Parish, T. S., & Taylor, J. (1979). The impact of divorce and subsequent father absence on children's and adolescent's self-concepts. *Journal of Youth and Adolescence, 8*, 427–432.

Parsons, T. (1968). The stability of the American family system. In N. W. Bell & E. F. Vogel (Eds.), *A modern introduction to the family*. New York: Free Press.

Pearlin, L. I., & Johnson, J. S. (1977). Marital status, life strains, and depression. *American Sociological Review, 42*, 704–715.

Pearson, J., & Thoennes, N. (1985). Child custody, child-support arrangements, and child-support payment patterns. *Juvenile and Family Court Journal, 14*, 49–56.

Pedro-Carroll, J. L., & Cowen, E. L. (1985). The Children of Divorce Intervention Program: An investigation of the efficacy of a school-based prevention program. *Journal of Consulting and Clinical Psychology, 53*, 603–611.

Pedro-Carroll, J. L., & Cowen, E. L. (in press). The Children of Divorce Intervention Program: Implementation and evaluation of a time-limited group approach. In J. P. Vincent (Ed.), *Advances in family intervention, assessment and theory* (vol. 4). Greenwich, CT: JAI.

Pedro-Carroll, J. L., Cowen, E. L., Hightower, A. D., & Guare, J. C. (1986). Preventive intervention with latency-aged children of divorce: A replication study. *American Journal of Community Psychology, 14*, 277–290.

Peters, M. F., & McAdoo, H. (1983). The present and future of alternative lifestyles in ethnic American cultures. In E. D. Macklin & R. H. Rubin (Eds.), *Contemporary families and alternative life styles* (pp. 288–307). Beverly Hills: Sage.

Peterson, J. L., & Zill, N. (1986). Marital disruption, parent-child relationships, and behavior problems in children. *Journal of Marriage and the Family, 48*, 295–307.

Phear, W.P.C., Beck, J. C., Hauser, B. B., Clark, S. C., & Whitney, R. A. (1984). An empirical study of custody agreements: Joint versus sole legal custody. In J. Folberg (Ed.), *Joint custody and shared parenting* (pp. 142–156). Washington: Bureau of National Affairs.

Plateris, A. (1974). 100 years of marriage and divorce statistics, 1867–1967. *Vital and Health Statistics*. Series 21, No. 24. DHEW Pub. No. (HRA) 74–1902. Health Resources Administration. Washington: U.S. Government Printing Office, Dec. 1973.

Pope, H., & Mueller, C. W. (1979). The intergenerational transmission of marital instability: Comparisons by race and sex. In G. Levinger & O. C. Moles, (Eds.), *Divorce and separation* (pp. 99–113). New York: Basic.

Porter, B., & O'Leary, K. D. (1980). Marital discord and childhood behavior problems. *Journal of Abnormal Child Psychology, 80*, 287–295.

Power, M. J., Ash, P. M. Schoenberg, E., & Sorey, E. C. (1974). Delinquency and the family. *British Journal of Social Work, 4*, 17–18.

Prinz, R. J., de Meyers, R., Holden, E. W., Tarnowski, K. J., & Roberts, W. A. (1983). Marital disturbance and child problems: A cautionary note regarding hyperactive children. *Journal of Abnormal Child Psychology, 11*, 393–399.

Raschke, H. J., & Raschke, V. J. (1979). Family conflict and children's self-concepts: A comparison of intact and single-parent families. *Journal of Marriage and the Family 41*, 367–374.

Rembar, J., Novick, J., Kalter, N. (1982). Attrition among families of divorce: Patterns in an out-patient psychiatric population. *Journal of the American Academy of Child Psychiatry, 21*, 409–413.

Rutter, M. (1971). Parent-child separation: Psychological effects on the children. *Journal of Child Psychology and Psychiatry, 12*, 233–260.

Rutter, M. (1981). *Maternal deprivation reassessed* (2nd Ed.). Harmondsworth: Penguin.

Rutter, M., & Giller, H. (1983). *Juvenile delinquency: Trends and perspectives.* New York: Guilford.

Rutter, M., & Quinton, D. (1984). Parental psychiatric disorder: Effects on children. *Psychological Medicine, 14*, 853–880.

Santrock, J. W. (1970). Paternal absence, sex-typing, and identification. *Developmental Psychology, 2*, 264–272.

Santrock, J. W. (1972). Relation of type and onset of father absence to cognitive development. *Child Development, 43*, 455–469.

Santrock, J. W., & Warshak, R. A. (1979). Father custody and social development in boys and girls. *Journal of Social Issues, 35*, 112–135.

Santrock, J. W., Warshak, R., Lindbergh, C., & Meadows, L. (1982). Children's and parents' observed social behavior in stepfather families. *Child Development, 53*, 472–480.

Scanzoni, J. (1979). A historical perspective on husband-wife bargaining power and marital dissolution. In G. Levinger & O. C. Moles (Eds.), *Divorce and separation* (pp. 20–36). New York: Basic.

Schneider, C. E. (1985). Moral discourse and the transformation of American family law. *Michigan Law Review, 83*, 1803–1880.

Scott, E. S., & Derdeyn, A. P. (1984). Rethinking joint custody. *Ohio State Law Journal, 45*, 455–474.

Select Committee on Children, Youth, and Families (SCCYF) of the United States House of Representatives (1983). *U.S. children and their families: Current conditions and recent trends.* Washington: Government Printing Office.

Shaw, D. S., & Emery, R. E. (1987). Parental conflict and the adjustment of school-age children whose parents have separated. *Journal of Abnormal Child Psychology, 15*, 269–281.

Shiller, V. M. (1986). Joint versus maternal custody for families with latency-age boys: Parent characteristics and child adjustment. *American Journal of Orthopsychiatry, 56*, 486–489.

Shinn, M. (1978). Father absence and children's cognitive development. *Psychological Bulletin, 85*, 295–324.

Slater, E. J., & Haber, J. D. (1984). Adolescent adjustment following divorce as a function of family conflict. *Journal of Consulting and Clinical Psychology, 52*, 920–921.

Spanier, G. B., & Anderson, E. A. (1979). Impact of the legal system on adjustment to marital separation. *Journal of Marriage and the Family, 41*, 605–613.

Sprenkle, D. H., & Storm, C. L. (1983). Divorce-therapy outcome research: A substantive and methodological review. *Journal of Marital and Family Therapy, 10*, 239–258.

Springer, C., & Wallerstein, J. S. (1983). Young adolescents' responses to their parents' divorces. In L. A. Kurdek (Ed.), *Children and divorce* (pp. 15–27). San Francisco: Jossey-Bass.

Steinberg, L. (1987). Single parents, stepparents, and the susceptibility of adolescents to antisocial peer pressure. *Child Development, 58,* 269–275.

Steinman, S. B., Zemmelman, S. E., & Knoblauch, T. M. (1985). A study of parents who sought joint custody following divorce: Who reaches agreement and sustains joint custody and who returns to court. *Journal of the American Academy of Child Psychiatry, 24,* 554–562.

Stolberg, A. L., & Anker, J. M. (1984). Cognitive and behavioral changes in children resulting from parental divorce and consequent environmental changes. *Journal of Divorce, 7,* 23–41.

Stolberg, A. L., Cullen, P. M., & Garrison, K. M. (1982). Divorce Adjustment Project: Preventive programming for children of divorce. *Journal of Preventive Psychiatry, 1* 365–368.

Stolberg, A. L., & Garrison, K. M. (1985). Evaluating a primary prevention program for children of divorce: The Divorce Adjustment Project. *American Journal of Community Psychology, 13,* 111–124.

Tennant, C., Bebbington, P., & Hurry, J. (1980). Parental death in childhood and risk of adult depressive disorders: A review. *Psychological Medicine, 10,* 289–299.

Thornton, A. (1977). Children and marital stability. *Journal of Marriage and the Family, 39,* 531–540.

Tuckman, J., & Regan, R. A. (1966). Intactness of the home and behavioral problems in children. *Journal of Child Psychology and Psychiatry, 7,* 225–233.

U.S. Bureau of the Census (1984). Marital status and living arrangements: March, 1983. *Current Population Reports* (Series P–20, No. 389). Washington: U.S. Department of Commerce.

Vuchinich, S., Emery, R. E., & Cassidy, J. (in press). Family members as third parties in dyadic family conflict: Strategies, alliances, and outcomes in family conflicts. *Child Development.*

Wadsworth, J. (1979). *Roots of delinquency.* New York: Barnes and Noble/Harper and Row.

Wadsworth, J. Burnell, Taylor, B., & Butler, N. (1985). The influence of family type on children's behavior and development at five years. *Journal of Child Psychology and Psychiatry, 26,* 245–254.

Wahler, R. G. (1980). The insular mother: Her problems in parent-child treatment. *Journal of Applied Behavior Analysis, 13,* 207–219.

Waite, L. J., Haggstrom, G. W., & Kanouse, D. E. (1985). The consequences of parenthood for the marital stability of young adults. *American Sociological Reivew, 50,* 850–857.

Waldron, H., & Routh, D. K. (1981). The effect of the first child on the marital relationship. *Journal of Marriage and the Family, 43,* 785–788.

Wallerstein, J. S. (1983). Children of divorce: The psychological tasks of childhood. *American Journal of Orthopsychiatry, 53,* 230–243.

Wallerstein. J. S. (1986). Children of divorce: Preliminary report of a ten-year follow-up of older chidren and adolescents. *Journal of the American Academy of Child Psychiatry, 24,* 545–553.

Wallerstein, J. S., & Kelly, J. B. (1980). *Surviving the breakup: How children actually cope with divorce.* New York: Basic.

Warshak, R. A. (1986). Father-custody and child development: A review and analysis of psychological research. *Behavioral Sciences and the Law 4,* 2–17.

Warshak, R. A., & Santrock, J. W. (1983). The impact of divorce in father-custody and mother-custody homes: The child's perspective. In L. A. Kurdek (Ed.), *Children and divorce* (pp. 29–46). San Francisco: Jossey-Bass.

Webster-Stratton, C. (1985). The effects of father involvement in parent training for conduct problem children. *Journal of Child Psychology and Psychiatry, 26*, 801–810.

Weiss, R. S. (1979a). Growing up a little faster: The experience of growing up in a single-parent household. *Journal of Social Issues, 35*, 97–111.

Weiss, R. S. (1979b). Issues in the adjudication of custody when parents separate. In G. Levinger & O. C. Moles (Eds.), *Divorce and separation* (pp. 324–336). New York: Basic.

Weitzman, L. J. (1981). *The marriage contract.* New York: Free Press.

Weitzman, L. J. (1981). The economics of divorce: Social and economic consequences of property, alimony, and child support awards. *UCLA Law Review, 28*, 1181–1268.

Weitzman, L. J. (1985). *The divorce revolution.* New York: Free Press.

Westman, J. D., Cline, D. W., Swift, W. J., & Kramer, D. A. (1970). The role of child psychiatry in divorce. *Archives of General Psychiatry, 23*, 416–420.

White, L. K., & Booth, A. (1985). The quality and stability of remarriage: The role of stepchildren. *American Sociological Review, 50*, 689–698.

Wolchik, S. A., Braver, S. L., & Sandler, I. W. (in press). Maternal versus joint custody: Children's postseparation experiences and adjustment. *Journal of Clinical Child Psychology.*

Wright, G. C., & Stetson, D. N. (1978). The impact of no-fault-divorce-law reform on divorce in American states. *Journal of Marriage and the Family, 40*, 575–580.

Young, E. R., & Parish, T. S. (1977). Impact of father absence during childhood on the psychological adjustment of college females. *Sex Roles, 3*, 217–227.

Zill, N. (1978, February). *Divorce, marital happiness, and the mental health of children: Findings from the FCD national survey of children.* Paper presented at the NIMH Workshop on Divorce and Children, Bethesda, Md.

SUBJECT INDEX

ABOUT THE AUTHOR

Robert E. Emery (Ph.D. SUNY at Stony Brook) is an Associate Professor of Psychology at the University of Virginia, where he teaches courses on childhood psychopathology, psychotherapy research, and divorce mediation. His numerous publications in the area of marital discord and divorce focus on children's adjustment, divorce mediation, and the process of conflict resolution. In addition to teaching and research, he is a practising clinical psychologist and mediator. This is his first book.